NORTH CAROLINA

in the

AMERICAN REVOLUTION

By

Hugh F. Rankin

Raleigh
North Carolina Department of Cultural Resources
Division of Archives and History
Fifth Printing
1982

Originally published in 1959 by the North Carolina Division of
Archives and History
ISBN 0-86526-091-5

FOR MY FATHER AND MOTHER

Who made it possible for me to grow up

in North Carolina

Major General Nathanael Greene of Rhode Island succeeded General Gates in command of the Continental army in the South, December, 1780.

CONTENTS

LIST OF ILLUSTRATIONS

FOREWORD

Over the years the Division of Archives and History has issued a series of pamphlets on North Carolina's role in the wars in which the United States has been involved. One of the most popular titles in this series has been Hugh F. Rankin's study of the American Revolution, originally published in 1959. This issuance marks the pamphlet's fifth printing. Dr. Rankin, a native of Rockingham County, teaches history at Tulane University in New Orleans, Louisiana. Miss Beth Crabtree, formerly a member of the Historical Publications Section's staff, edited the pamphlet, selected and arranged the illustrations, and saw the manuscript through press.

The pictures in the pamphlet came from several sources. Nine pictures are from Benson J. Lossing's *The Pictorial Field Book of the Revolution*, Volume II: Robert Howe, p. 523; Sir Henry Clinton, p. 556; Francis Marion, p. 478; Isaac Shelby, p. 425; Horatio Gates, p. 463; Henry Lee, p. 385; O. H. Williams, p. 396; Cornwallis's Headquarters, p. 575; and Cornwallis's Surrender at Yorktown, p. 319. Three pictures, from the Albert Barden Collection in the Division of Archives and History, are those of Nathanael Greene, George III, and Joseph McDowell. The Battle of King's Mountain is from *A Complete History of the United States of America*, by J. A. Spence, Volume 1, p. 83. The prints of Abner Nash, William Richardson Davie, Joseph Hewes, and William Hooper are from negatives in the Division of Archives and History. Prints of all of the pictures listed above were made by Mrs. Madlin Futrell, formerly a member of the staff of the Museum Section. The print of Banastre Tarleton was made by the photoduplication service of the University Library, Chapel Hill. Dr. Rankin furnished the print of Lord Cornwallis, taken from the *London Magazine*, June, 1781; he also supplied the print of Daniel Morgan, from an original painting by Chappel. The map came from Miss Susan Armstrong of Colonial Williamsburg.

Memory F. Mitchell
Historical Publications Administrator

June 1, 1982

Chapter I

WAR COMES TO NORTH CAROLINA

Governor Josiah Martin was an angry man. Not only was he outraged, but he felt he had been mistreated. He had tried to govern the colony of North Carolina to the best of his ability, and he had been a faithful servant of his King, George III of England. Now he was caught in a movement more powerful than kings, a movement that was pulling him down into a great whirlpool of fury and hatred towards the British Empire. Governor Martin could not be held responsible for the spirit of rebellion spreading like an infectious disease throughout the colony; it was not of his doing—but it was his duty to stop it, if he could.

Actually, the people in all of the thirteen American colonies had become disgruntled and restless long before Governor Martin's arrival in North Carolina in 1771. The trouble had started in the legislative body of England—the British Parliament. Back in 1763, the English Government had needed money. They had just finished fighting the long and expensive Seven Years' War with France, a dreary piece of business that the colonists had called the French and Indian War.

Wars cost money and usually drain a country of its wealth. Since the British Government had spent money and sent soldiers to protect the Americans from the French and the Indians, they now felt that it was only right for the colonies to help pay the cost of the war. Acts were passed in the British Parliament placing taxes on certain American activities. Many of these laws concerned trade. North Carolina did not have the harbors or the background to develop a trading economy, and most of these early acts affected the colony very little. But the Royal Proclamation of 1763, the Sugar Act of 1764, the Currency Act of 1764, and the Quartering Act of 1765 were felt by the other colonies, especially the trading colonies to the north. As a matter of principle, the North Carolina Assembly, or legislature, protested that Parliament had no right to tax the colonies. Only the colonial legislatures, they declared, could tax the colonies.

In the spring of 1765 word was received that the British Parliament had passed a law that would affect greatly the daily life of the North Carolinians and of all the other colonists.

This was the famous Stamp Act. Nearly every person would feel the effects of the act. For instance, no newspaper could be sold unless it bore the official stamp. Men and women could no longer get married unless their marriage license had been stamped. A student could not even graduate from one of the few colleges in America unless he paid a fee to have the stamp affixed to his diploma. Even more irritating and expensive, all papers used in business transactions had to bear the despised stamp.

The people of North Carolina joined the other colonists in violent protest. Down on the coast, in the port of Brunswick, government officials seized two ships whose papers had not been stamped. A milling throng of shouting people forced them to release the ships. In some colonies officials were not allowed to distribute the stamps. In others, the people refused to purchase stamps and went about their daily business as if nothing had happened. Great mobs of people in some colonies shouted their disapproval of the Stamp Act. The men who dared to defy the might of the British Empire called themselves the "Sons of Liberty." So effective were the protests that the British Parliament repealed the Stamp Act in 1766. There was rejoicing in all the colonies, with people joining in parades and other celebrations. Some of them actually began to feel a little cocky because they felt that they had forced mighty England to back down. In their happiness, few of the colonists noticed that at the same time Parliament had repealed the Stamp Act, another piece of legislation had been passed. This was the Declaratory Act, which stated in no uncertain terms that the British Parliament had the right to tax the colonies any time they saw fit.

The colonists had little time to gloat over their victory. In the summer of 1767, Parliament struck back with the passage of the Townshend Acts. These laws placed a tax on many of the necessities of life. Again the Americans, including the people of North Carolina, raised their voices in protest. The cry of "No taxation without representation" began to echo throughout the colonies. No colonists sat in the British Parliament, therefore they were not represented and the taxes imposed by the British legislature were illegal. Only their own representatives, elected by the qualified voters in the colonies and sitting in the colonial legislatures, had the right to tax the people of America. Thus the people drew together in their opposition to England.

They refused to buy goods manufactured by the British. And the Parliament again backed down. In March, 1770, all of the Townshend taxes were repealed except the tax on tea.

Governor Martin had arrived in North Carolina in 1771. This new governor was a young man, ambitious, and extremely anxious to do a good job in the service of his King. To the casual observer, things appeared quiet. But even a late arrival like Josiah Martin could soon see that the people were restless—they appeared to be waiting for the next move by Parliament.

Men were going quietly about the colony organizing the people. They bore names to remember: Cornelius Harnett, John Harvey, Robert Howe, Richard Caswell, Alexander Lillington, Edward Vail, John Ashe, Joseph Hewes, Samuel Johnston, Edward Buncombe, William Hooper, and James and Maurice Moore. These men, and others like them, were trying to set up an organization to hold North Carolina together in the event there was a break with England—a break that many felt was sure to come. Some were selected to serve in groups known as "Committees of Correspondence." These committees communicated with similar groups in other colonies, and kept each other informed of latest developments in their neighborhoods. They also began to work up plans of action when and if the anticipated break with England should come. It should be kept in mind that there was no national government in America at this time. Each of the thirteen colonies had a separate government. But a spirit of unity was being built up through the activities of the Committees of Correspondence.

When the break with the Mother Country finally did come, it occurred far from North Carolina. The East India Company, one of the great English trading companies of that day, was in trouble. Their warehouses in England had great stores of unsold tea. To help the company unload this surplus, Parliament gave it the exclusive right to sell tea in the American colonies. The New England colonies—Massachusetts, Connecticut, Rhode Island, and New Hampshire—were engaged in commercial activities. Their very existence depended upon the goods they could sell and carry in their ships. This act by the British government angered these northern merchants. They felt that no English company had a right to the profits to be found in the colonies. And besides, if one monopoly were granted, monopolies could likewise be given to other English companies.

This resentment eventually was expressed in violent action. On a chilly December night in 1773, a group of Boston citizens, poorly disguised as Mohawk Indians, marched down to the wharves. There they boarded a British ship, and working swiftly and quietly, they dumped 342 chests of British tea into Boston harbor. This seemed to set a pattern. Similar "tea parties," although on a smaller scale, were held in other colonies. The patriotic ladies of Edenton, North Carolina, did their bit by vowing to drink no more of the detested British tea.

The British government was in no mood to sit by idly and allow such actions to go unpunished. To them, the colonies were like the children of the British Empire. When children are naughty, they should be spanked. Punishment for the Americans took the form of the so-called "Coercive Acts." The Port of Boston was closed to all trade, and a number of restrictions were placed upon the colonial government of Massachusetts. Although these acts were designed primarily to punish the people of Massachusetts, many felt that the same sort of restrictions could be placed on any colony in America. Angry people in every colony held meetings of protest. Aid was sent to Boston. From North Carolina sailed the ship, "Penelope," laden with a cargo of corn, flour, and pork to help feed the citizens of the Massachusetts town.

It was obvious to most thinking people that a break could take place between England and the colonies at almost any moment. Even more important, they realized that so powerful a nation as Great Britain could easily conquer the colonies by striking them one at a time. Then, too, no protest would carry much weight with Parliament unless it were a protest by all the colonies. They had to strengthen themselves through some form of union. Messengers, clattering along forest roads on swift horses, brought the word that Virginia and Massachusetts were calling upon the other colonies to join them and present a united front to England. Each colony was to select delegates to represent them in a Congress. Because it was to contain representatives from all the English-speaking colonies on the continent of North America, it was to be called the "Continental Congress."

When Governor Martin heard of this meeting, he resolved to do everything within his power to prevent the people of North Carolina from sending delegates. Say what you will about Josiah Martin, he was a devoted servant of his King. And it was his responsibility to put a stop to anything against the interests of his Sovereign. He threw every possible legal obstacle in the path of those who would oppose the British government. He refused to issue a call for a meeting of the North Carolina Assembly, which was supposed to elect the delegates to the Congress. No Assembly—no delegates.

But the governor was dealing with an aroused populace; people who felt their rights had been trampled into the dust. Such men were determined that no mere royal governor would stand in their way. On August 25, 1774, representatives of the people met in a Provincial Congress in New Bern—the very town in which the Governor's Palace was located. These defiant, but still respectful, men drew up a statement in which they declared they still recognized George III as their rightful Sovereign, but they heatedly denied the right of the British Parliament to tax them. Only the North Carolina Assembly, they argued, had that right. In addition to this declaration, they also drew up an agreement stating that they would no longer buy from or sell to British merchants. Having stated clearly where they stood in the dispute with England, these men elected William Hooper, Richard Caswell, and Joseph Hewes to represent North Carolina in the Continental Congress. Josiah Martin did not realize it, but he was no longer the governor of North Carolina. True, he still held the title, and he still occupied the Governor's Palace, but he had lost control over the people of the colony.

Nevertheless, Governor Martin fought hard for his King. He used every trick he knew to try to bring the North Carolinians back into line. He called a meeting of the Assembly, perhaps feeling that he could persuade them to reconsider their rash ideas. The members of the Assembly had other plans. The day before the Assembly was to meet, they met in another Provincial Congress. This unauthorized meeting brought harsh words from the governor. The Congress, in turn, replied in words equally harsh and bitter. After this exchange of mutual disrespect, the Provincial Congress issued a statement of vibrant independence. In this they asserted the right of the people to hold meetings and to present their complaints to the King.

Almost immediately after adjourning as a Provincial Congress, the same men reassembled as the North Carolina Assembly. In fact, they acted as though they were the Provincial Congress repeating themselves. Certainly, insofar as Martin was concerned, they were no better than the Congress. He was furious as they repeated almost the same statements they had issued as a Congress. As governor, Josiah Martin had the right to prorogue, or dismiss, the Assembly whenever he felt they were overstepping their authority. This he did now, feeling that they had insulted his royal master, and that he had to do something to bring the people of North Carolina back into line.

Even as the governor racked his brain for a method by which he could halt this tide of rebellion, events in faraway Massachusetts made his task virtually impossible. Under the command of General Thomas Gage, British soldiers had been stationed in Boston. General Gage had received orders to collect all arms and ammunition which might be used against British troops, if fighting did break out. The people of Massachusetts had stored military supplies in the little towns of Lexington and Concord, not too far from Boston. On the night of April 18, 1775, British soldiers slipped quietly out of the city, hoping to take these supplies without trouble. Riders in the night, led by a round-faced Boston silversmith named Paul Revere, galloped through the countryside, warning militia and minutemen that the redcoats were on the march. In the early morning of April 19th, on the village greens of Lexington and Concord, the British were temporarily brought to a halt by the determined citizens of these towns. Muskets were fired; men dropped to the ground. The British charged with the bayonet, and then marched on. These few scattered shots on two tiny village greens were not really a battle. Nevertheless, they started a war, and so important were the results that the poet Emerson immortalized them as "the shot heard 'round the world."

It was some time before the people of North Carolina heard of this skirmish. In 1775 news traveled slowly, on foot, horseback, or by boat. Even riders astride the fastest horses did not bring the news of the battles of Lexington and Concord to North Carolina until late May. Then the North Carolinians, as did the other colonists, began to clean their rifles and muskets and to check their ammunition. Now they had to fight or else forsake their fellow colonists in the north to the fury of British vengeance.

People in the vicinity of Charlotte in Mecklenburg County were as mad as hornets. In May, 1775, they held a meeting. Out of this meeting came ringing resolutions declaring that the officers of the King no longer held any authority in North Carolina. Anyone who thought otherwise, they said, would be considered an enemy to his country. They also urged the people to elect military officers who held no affection for Great Britain.

All over North Carolina men began to choose sides. Those who had rebelled against the authority of the King of England called themselves the "Whigs." Others, who could not bring themselves to rebel against their King, were referred to as loyalists, or more often, "Tories." Still others remained neutral as long as they could, supporting neither one side nor the other.

It was obvious that angry words would be followed by the louder sounds of muskets and rifles. To keep his family from harm, Governor Martin sent his wife and children to New York. He set up a half dozen cannon before the Palace in New Bern. The same night, these were taken away quietly by the Whigs. The governor was determined that the remaining cannon should not be used against British soldiers. He therefore ruined them by driving iron spikes through the touch holes so that they no longer could be fired. Under the protection of a dark night, he buried his powder and shot in the cellar and beneath the cabbage bed in the garden. Then, alarmed at the growing spirit of rebellion, he fled to the protection of Fort Johnston on the Cape Fear River.

Fort Johnston offered little protection. It was badly in need of repair and there was only a small supply of ammunition. Several of the soldiers stationed there flatly refused to fight against their friends and neighbors. They left quietly at the first opportunity. Nevertheless, Governor Martin, who at one time had been an officer in the British army, began to make preparations to defend himself.

The flight of the governor had left the colony without a legal government. Groups called "Committees of Safety" began to take over. They were organized in every community as a means of keeping law and order, and to raise men to fight the British. When the Wilmington Committee of Safety discovered that Governor Martin had taken refuge within Fort Johnston, they realized something had to be done to prevent its becoming a British stronghold. A strong fort could offer protection to soldiers being landed from British warships. It was with this possibility in mind that the Wilmington Committee of Safety sent out a call for men to aid in the destruction of the fort. Still not too sure of the legality of their own position, they also sent a letter to Governor Martin, informing him that they planned to destroy the fortifications and take the cannon for their own use.

Martin was no fool in military matters. He was not rash enough to believe he could defend the fort with his small garrison. Neither did he have time to make all the necessary repairs. He removed the cannon from their carriages, and then ordered that all the ammunition and supplies be rowed out to the "Cruizer," a small British warship anchored in the river. From the deck of this vessel he watched a large group of rebels under the command of Robert Howe, Cornelius Harnett, and John Ashe approach the walls of the fort. A short time later, flames leaping up into the hot July sky told him that Fort Johnston soon would be no more than a pile of smoke-blackened timbers and ashes.

The burning of the fort indicated that the people of eastern North Carolina had made their choice. This act of defiance had transformed them from loyal subjects of George III into rebels against His Majesty's government. On August 8, 1775, Governor Martin issued a fiery proclamation which he hoped would be read by most of the people of the colony. In this he angrily accused the Committees of Safety of being responsible for the destruction of Fort Johnston. The Wilmington Committee, he said, was the worst of the lot. Yet, on the other hand, he felt that most of the people of North Carolina still retained their allegiance to the King. But what the royal governor really needed was men with guns. Words scratched out with a goose quill pen are not half so effective as bullets.

On the other side of the fence were the patriots, or as Martin called them, the rebels. These men felt the need for some stronger government than the local Committees of Safety. With this thought in mind they called for a second Provincial Congress to meet in Hillsboro on August 20, 1775. As soon as they were assembled the Congress elected Samuel Johnston of Chowan County as their president and presiding officer. For the next three weeks this Congress sat in Hillsboro. One of the first things that every member did was to sign a "test oath," stating that despite the ill feeling existing between England and the colonies, the members of this Congress were still loyal to George III. But, they declared, no part of the British government had the right to impose taxes on the American colonies without the consent of the colonists.

Despite these statements of loyalty, the members of the Congress voted to take steps to purchase arms and ammunition. Money had to be raised to pay for the weapons. They also replied to Governor Martin's proclamation of August 8th with a statement of their own. They pointed out that the governor was really attempting to set the people of North Carolina against each other. Because of this, they ordered Martin's proclamation taken to some public place and there burned by the public hangman.

To prevent the colony from falling to pieces, a Committee of Safety was organized for the whole of North Carolina. This group of thirteen members was to perform the same functions for which the governor had formerly been responsible. The Congress also provided for the enlistment of an army of 10,000 men, and considered ways to raise the money with which to pay these soldiers. They urged that 10,000 "minutemen" be organized, ready to answer the call to arms at a moment's notice. Thus did the colony prepare for war.

War in 1775, as always, was an ugly business. No one wanted to suffer the hardships that came with soldiering, nor did any want to run the risk of being killed. Yet these men of North Carolina believed so strongly in their rights as a free people that they were willing to fight and even die for them. It was in this spirit and with these ideals that the leaders of North Carolina prepared their people for war.

CHAPTER II

THE BATTLE AT MOORE'S CREEK BRIDGE

The powder smoke above the villages of Lexington and Concord soon drifted away on the early morning breeze, but the shooting had just begun. The British soldiers had to fight their way back into Boston and to the safety of their fortifications. From behind every stone wall and nearly every tree along the way, the farmers of Massachusetts poured a leaden hail of bullets into their columns. The British found no rest in Boston. The people of New England, angry beyond all description, began to gather in a great army around the city. Earthworks were thrown up by busy shovels. Soon the booming of cannon and the crack of muskets announced to the world that the American colonies were now determined to throw off the yoke of British rule. From other colonies men came marching to lend a hand to the people of Massachusetts.

Robert Howe of Brunswick County served as a commander of a regiment of North Carolina troops in the Continental army. Howe was promoted from colonel to brigadier general and then to major general in command of the troops in the South. He was the highest ranking North Carolinian in the Continental army.

The Second Continental Congress assembled in Philadelphia on May 10, 1775. They were faced with a multitude of tasks—securing supplies, raising troops, and selecting a general to command their army. For commander-in-chief they chose a tall, silent planter from Virginia, George Washington. The Congress also required each colony to recruit, equip, and train a specified number of soldiers. These were to be included within a military force known as the "Continental Army," to be under the command of General Washington. North Carolina was to raise two regiments, one under the command of Colonel James Moore of New Hanover County, the other under Colonel Robert Howe of Brunswick County.

Governor Josiah Martin had no intention of allowing these things to come to pass in North Carolina. He too had been making plans. Every day, and sometimes far into the night, his goose quill pen had been busily scratching out plans and letters for the authorities in England. He wrote to Thomas Gage, the British general in Boston, asking for weapons and ammunition. To England he sent a plan which he felt would result not only in defeating the rebels of North Carolina, but would also be useful in taking South Carolina. Charleston, South Carolina, at this time was the most prosperous and important seaport in the South. If the British could take this town, the task of conquering the southern colonies would be made much easier.

Charles, Earl Cornwallis, was the other British commander sent to assist in putting down the rebellion in the South. He succeeded Clinton upon the latter's return to New York following his successful campaign against Charleston.

In his letters to British government officials, Governor Martin had declared that he would be able to raise an army of North Carolinians who would fight alongside the British redcoats. So convincing were his letters, the British authorities decided to use some of his plans. They replied that early in 1776 two fleets, with two British armies on board, would drop anchor in the Cape Fear River. One of these would be coming from Boston under the command of Sir Henry Clinton. The other army would be sailing from Ireland with its general, Lord Charles Cornwallis. They were to meet off the coast of North Carolina, where they were to be joined by the troops of Governor Martin. The combined force would then take Charleston. After that, they thought, they could roll over the remaining southern colonies.

Josiah Martin was confident that he could recruit at least 3,000 loyal troops in North Carolina. Some of these he hoped to enlist from among the "Regulators." These people, from the neighborhoods of Hillsboro and Salisbury, were still angry because of their defeat at the Battle of Alamance in 1771 by the people of the eastern part of North Carolina under the command of Governor William Tryon. Because the revolutionary leaders of North Carolina were from the eastern section, Martin felt that the Regulators would have nothing to do with the movement.

Other loyal troops, he felt, could be enlisted among the Scotch Highlanders who had settled in the Cape Fear section of the colony. In 1746 they had revolted against the King of England and led by "Bonnie Prince Charlie," they had been defeated in the Battle of Culloden. After that, and before they migrated to the New World, they had taken an oath of allegiance to the King of England. And these Highlanders were people who believed in keeping their word. They had settled in eastern North Carolina around Cross Creek (present-day Fayetteville) and Cross Hill (present-day Carthage). Some had become prosperous merchants. Others had earned a good living by producing naval stores (tar, pitch, and turpentine) used in the construction of ships for the British navy.

Sir Henry Clinton sailed from England with his troops and, upon Governor Josiah Martin's request for aid, anchored off the Cape Fear River. Too late to aid the loyalists at Moore's Creek Bridge, Clinton continued to Charleston, South Carolina, where he was driven off by the South Carolinians. Later, on May 12, 1780, he forced the surrender of the city.

General Gage sent two regular British army officers to aid Governor Martin in training and organizing his loyal troops. These two men, Lieutenant Colonel Donald MacDonald and Captain Donald McLeod, both originally from Scotland, were good choices for the job. They came ashore near New Bern. They had discarded their uniforms and were dressed in civilian clothes, but the New Bern Committee of Safety had heard they were coming. The two Scottish officers were good actors. When they were called before the Committee, they were so persuasive in their tales that the Committee not only allowed them to go their way, but also warned them against the activities of Governor Martin.

As soon as Martin heard of their arrival, he made MacDonald a brigadier general and McLeod a lieutenant colonel in the loyalist militia. A call was sent out for all loyalists to come to Cross Hill or Cross Creek. Some drifted in, but others were not able to answer the call of the governor. Some had been driven from their homes by the rebels and were hiding out in the forests. Others, marching to Cross Creek, were driven back by the Whigs, as the rebels were now beginning to call themselves. Some were rounded up and clapped into jail. Others were just too frightened and stayed home. Some had even arrived at Cross Creek, only to decide the governor did not have much of an army, and had returned to their homes. The Tory army, nevertheless, increased.

All this activity in and around Cross Creek had not escaped the attention of the Whigs. They too began to move towards that town. They were a strange appearing group. They marched along, ill-trained men in rough clothes, to the rattle of a not too well-beat drum, and occasionally even to the whine and screech of an ill-played fiddle. Two more soldierly units, the two Continental regiments under Colonels Moore and Howe, also began to move towards Cross Creek. Colonel James Moore, as senior officer present, assumed the command of all the patriot troops.

Governor Martin tried to draw attention away from his troops at Cross Hill. The warship "Cruizer" was sent up the Cape Fear as a threat. At Wilmington the ugly muzzles of cannon jutting over the tops of hastily thrown-up earthworks frightened the sailors and they turned back. When the ship put a raiding party over the side, rifle fire from both sides of the river sent the men hastily rowing back to the protection of their ship. These same rifles kept popping away as the "Cruizer" dropped back down the river. This little incident made it clear that the governor could not hope to send aid to MacDonald by way of the Cape Fear River.

At Cross Creek, General MacDonald was trying desperately to whip his Tory army into shape. Reports were that the Whigs were closing in fast. He now had around 1,400 men under his command, but only 520 of them were armed. All available muskets and rifles were collected from the neighborhood. One man, who possessed some skill with a needle, was put to work sewing a British battle flag of red, white, and blue cloth.

On February 18, 1776, General MacDonald gave the orders to march. His Tory army didn't travel very far. Only seven miles out of Cross Creek, at a place called Rockfish Creek, they were brought to a halt. Just across the creek were Colonel James Moore and 2,000 Whig soldiers. MacDonald tried to bluff his way through. He sent a note to Moore threatening severe punishment to the rebels, if they didn't surrender to the troops of the King. Moore gave as good as he took, and his notes were just as threatening as those of his enemy. Moore was playing for time, hoping to delay MacDonald until reinforcements could come up.

MacDonald had to do something and do it quickly. He knew that Moore's troops outnumbered his and the longer he waited the more Whigs would join his enemy. When the possibility of a battle had been suggested, some of his Tories had quietly picked up their arms and had faded quickly among the trees. He now decided to try to outwit Moore by slipping away and trying another route to the sea. He drew up his troops in formation and began to speak. His voice grew bolder and louder as he called upon those men who were not ready to die for their cause to say so then and now. Twenty men, who admitted their "Courage was not Warproof," sheepishly stepped forward out of the ranks. Laying down their arms amidst the jeers of their former comrades, they fled into the shelter of the nearby trees. There was no such cowardice among the remaining Tory troops. When MacDonald had finished his fiery speech, they gave three mighty cheers as they marched away.

Almost back to Cross Creek the Tories marched. There they loaded into boats and rowed across the Cape Fear River. On the other side, the boats were destroyed to delay any pursuit. They then turned east and began the long march towards the coast.

MacDonald had outwitted Moore. It was not until the next morning that the Whigs discovered the absence of the enemy. Colonel James Moore was not a man to sit around and mope because he had been outmaneuvered by an intelligent enemy, and now he moved fast. Some of the troops under his command were directed to occupy Cross Creek. This prevented the Tories from having a base to which they could return. Moore had received word that troops under the command of Colonel Richard Caswell were marching from New Bern. He ordered these men to change their line of march and take a position at Corbett's Ferry on the Black River. Other troops were to try to reinforce Caswell at that place. If this was impossible, they were to station themselves at the bridge crossing the Widow Moore's Creek, just seventeen miles from Wilmington. Moore led his own troops to Elizabeth Town to block that road to the sea.

While all of this was going on, MacDonald's army gradually was pushing its way through the wilderness. The wagons carrying supplies creaked slowly across the rough terrain. Bridges had to be braced to hold the heavy loads. Patrols constantly had to scour the countryside to prevent an ambush by the enemy. On February 23, three days after he had left Rockfish Creek, MacDonald reached Corbett's Ferry on the Black River.

General MacDonald had planned to use the ferry to cross the river. A five-man patrol scouting for Caswell was captured. From it he learned that Caswell and his men were waiting for him on the other side of the stream. The Tory general's only hope was to outwit Caswell just as he had outwitted Moore. A small group of men were left at the ferry while the main body of his men marched upstream. Those who remained kept out of sight, but they were extremely noisy. They tramped through the woods, shouting to each other. Some beat drums; others played shrill tunes on the bagpipes. Still others concealed themselves along the river bank and sent an occasional rifle shot whining across the stream to prevent Caswell's men from becoming too curious. On the other side, Caswell thought MacDonald's entire army was getting ready to try a crossing. He ordered his men to dig in.

Upstream, MacDonald, using this extra time, completed a bridge across the river. By eight o'clock on the morning of February 26th his men had made the crossing and once again were on the march.

Colonel Caswell soon discovered that he had been led astray by a few bagpipes, drums, and rifle shots. He immediately led his troops on a fast march to get to Moore's Creek Bridge ahead of the Tories. When he arrived, he discovered that Colonel Alexander Lillington was already on the ground and had begun to throw up earthworks. Caswell crossed to the other side and began to dig in with his back to the creek.

MacDonald drove his men, but when he was within six miles of the bridge he learned from his scouts that Caswell had won the race. He sent a messenger into the camp of the enemy to demand Caswell's surrender. Actually, MacDonald knew that Caswell had no intention of surrendering, but the messenger had been sent to spy. When he returned he reported to the Tory general that Caswell had encamped on the near side of the bridge, with his back to the creek.

MacDonald was an old man and the strain of the forced march overcame him. Finding that he was now too ill to lead his troops into battle, he called his officers to his bedside. They were confident they could defeat the rebels and wanted to attack early enough next morning to surprise Caswell's men as they still lay sleeping around their campfires. The sick general then appointed Lieutenant Colonel Donald McLeod to lead the assault.

Early that evening, rifles, muskets, and ammunition were checked. A number of the Tories had no firearms, but they were prepared to go into battle swinging their claymores, the traditional broadsword of the Scotch Highlanders. At one o'clock in the morning they began the march towards the enemy camp.

It was dark. Clouds scudding across the sky obscured the faint light of the moon and the stars. The Tories lost their way and spent much of their time floundering in the muck and mire of the swamps. A little before dawn they saw the fires of Caswell's camp flickering through the trees. Silently, the Tories formed themselves into three columns. Just as silently they entered the Whig camp, ready to pounce upon the sleeping enemy. There was no enemy! During the night Caswell had pulled back across the creek to join Lillington's troops, leaving his campfires burning to confuse the Tories. The tables were turned. This time the Whigs had outwitted the Tories. Now the Tories had to attempt an assault across the bridge.

McLeod pulled his troops back into the shelter of the trees to form for the attack. A rallying cry, "King George and Broad Swords," was passed along the line. Three cheers were to be the signal for the attack. They waited for the first signs of dawn. Suddenly, there was a burst of rifle fire near the bridge. McLeod decided to wait no longer, although it was not yet daylight. Three cheers rang out, drums began to roll, and the shrill squeal of

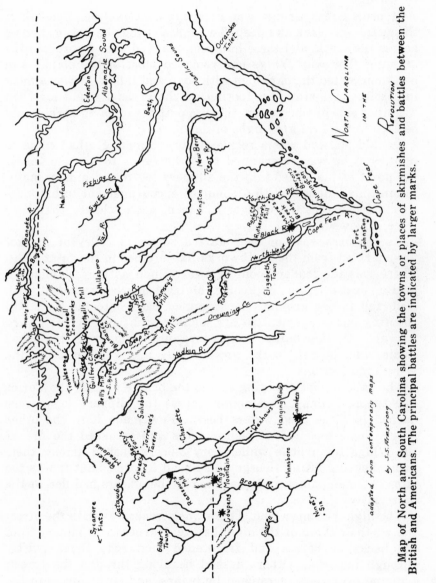

Map of North and South Carolina showing the towns or places of skirmishes and battles between the British and Americans. The principal battles are indicated by larger marks.

bagpipes cut through the cool morning air. The line moved forward.

Moore's Creek Bridge was of crude construction. Beneath it the water was dark and deep. Two massive logs had been thrown across the creek, and these had been planked over to provide the crossing. The wily Whigs had removed most of the planks and had then coated the bare logs with soap and tallow. It was almost impossible to maintain a footing on the greasy, round logs. On the other side of the stream, the dim outlines of earthworks could be seen in the first gray light of dawn.

Donald McLeod was a recklessly brave man. He had come to fight, and he was determined to do battle or to die. He thrust the point of his sword into the slippery log to aid him in maintaining his balance. With a shout of encouragement to his men, he started across the bridge. His men, good soldiers that they were, followed.

As the first wave of men started across, a volley of musket fire sparkled from the earthworks like fireflies in the faint light. There was the louder boom of two cannon as they slammed a load of death across the bridge. McLeod, his body riddled with lead, fell to the ground. He struggled back onto his feet, still shouting encouragement to his soldiers and pointing his sword forward. Another hail of bullets tore into the body of this brave soldier and he fell to the ground only a few paces from the Whig fortifications.

The rain of shot sweeping across the bridge toppled the Tories like tenpins. Many, scrambling across the slippery logs, were dashed into the deep waters below. Few made it to the other shore. Some took refuge behind trees and returned the fire of the Whigs for a little while. Tory officers dashed among their men, shouting "King George and Broad Swords," but it was too late. The men panicked. Even some of the officers had fled at the first volley.

The flight became a rout. There was a general rush in the direction of their camp of the night before. Harness was ripped from the backs of horses and frightened men rode them swiftly through the trees. Others dashed headlong through the forest, tripping over roots, scratched by briars, and sprawling into the murky waters of the swamps.

As the Tories fled, the Whigs leaped over their fortifications with shouts of victory. For a short distance they pursued the

Tories. But the battle was over. Some say it lasted for only about three minutes. In that short interval, only two of the men under Caswell and Lillington had been wounded, and only one of them later died of his wounds. At least thirty of the Tories had been killed, but it was estimated that many more later died of their wounds.

The Tories covered the six miles back to their camp at a much faster pace than they had marched to battle only a few hours earlier. They found their sick general, MacDonald, still sleeping peacefully in his tent, unaware of the disaster which had overtaken his little army. The remaining officers held a hasty council of war. As the Whigs now blocked their return to Cross Creek, they decided to divide their remaining ammunition and make their way back to their homes as best they could. To protect themselves, they decided to march in a group for a portion of the way. General MacDonald, still too weak to travel, was left in his tent.

Back at the battlefield, Caswell and Lillington had been joined by Colonel James Moore. Moore assumed command and organized the troops for the pursuit of the enemy. Scouting parties soon were roaming the countryside in search of the fugitives. MacDonald was among the first to be captured. He was taken to New Bern and later to Halifax, where he was placed in jail.

MacDonald's Tory army soon suffered the same fate as their commanding officer. They had marched but a little distance when they were suddenly surrounded by mounted Whigs. They surrendered without firing a shot. About 850 of the privates were allowed to return to their homes after promising they would not fight again. The officers were taken to Halifax and there placed in the same jail as their general.

The Tory thrust had been put down, but Governor Josiah Martin could not bring himself to believe it. He was still aboard the "Cruizer," still writing letters to the officials in the British government. The defeat at Moore's Creek Bridge, he said, was really nothing to worry about. Future plans were sure to work out and North Carolina would once again become a British colony.

The people of North Carolina felt differently. They felt the victory settled once and for all the question of any danger from the Tories. The Whigs, now feeling safe, and perhaps a little cocky, began to persecute the loyalists. Many of those who still favored the King were forced to hide in the swamps and forests in fear of their lives. There was continued fighting around New England and New York, but those places were far, far away. It appeared to be all over in North Carolina. It wasn't, and the Whigs were due for a rude awakening.

In May, 1776, war seemed to have come again to North Carolina. The British fleet carrying the troops of Sir Henry Clinton and Lord Cornwallis dropped anchor in the Cape Fear River. They had been scheduled to arrive in February, but heavy seas and winter storms had delayed their arrival. Had they arrived on time, the battle of Moore's Creek Bridge might have had a different ending. Now, to the Whigs, their arrival appeared to be an invasion of North Carolina. They began to arm themselves again and calls for aid were sent to the sister colonies of Virginia and South Carolina.

They had little to fear. The original British plans called for the Tories to join the British fleet. Instead of a victorious Tory army, the British generals found only an angry Josiah Martin sulking aboard the "Cruizer." Some landing parties were put ashore to make raids along the river. A few houses were plundered of their valuables and some of the plantation homes along the river were burned. That was about all the damage the British were able to do, for they soon weighed anchor and sailed south for an attack on Charleston, South Carolina.

The North Carolinians had overcome their first obstacle on the road to independence. They had played havoc with the scheme of a royal governor, and they had defeated their enemies in a pitched battle. The threat of British invasion seemed more remote than ever after the South Carolinians had driven the British fleet away from Charleston. Now they were free to establish a government of free men.

CHAPTER III

A NEW STATE AND NEW PROBLEMS

A provisional government had been established by the Congress which met at Halifax in August 1775, but that government was only temporary. All the political leaders of the colony realized that a more permanent form of government was necessary. This was impossible, however, so long as North Carolina remained a colony, her people subjects of the King of England. Technically, they were still members of the British Empire, and could do nothing towards establishing a permanent government until they had declared themselves independent. This situation existed in all thirteen colonies, but it was North Carolina who unlocked the gates of independence.

On April 4, 1776, another Provincial Congress met in Halifax. The delegates to this assembly were brave men, their confidence partially inspired by the victory at Moore's Creek Bridge. Although they may not have realized it, they were now to take the biggest political step of their lives. On April 12, 1776 (a day to remember), this Congress adopted a resolution which has since become known as the Halifax Resolves. The Provincial Congress of North Carolina instructed their delegates to the Continental Congress to concur, or agree, with any action that might be taken towards independence. This was the first giant step toward independence taken by any colony. In a sense, it was a suggestion to the Continental Congress that it make a similar move.

Virginia took the next step. On May 15, 1776, the Virginia Provincial Congress, meeting in Williamsburg, instructed its delegates in the Continental Congress to propose independence. In the meantime, the North Carolina delegation had arrived in Philadelphia and had laid their instructions before the Continental Congress. The instruction that they concur in any move toward independence was received with enthusiasm by the delegates from the other colonies.

On a warm June 7, 1776, Richard Henry Lee of Virginia rose from his seat in the Congress. In a voice loud and firm he proposed "that these United Colonies are, and of right ought to be free and independent states. . . ." After some debate, the resolution was adopted and a committee was selected to draw up a declaration of independence. Thomas Jefferson of Virginia wrote most of the document, but he was aided by Benjamin Franklin of Pennsylvania, John Adams of Massachusetts, Robert Livingston of New York, and Roger Sherman of Connecticut. On July 2,

1776, the Continental Congress voted that from this time forward the American colonies would be independent states. Two days later, on July 4, 1776, they adopted the Declaration of Independence. William Hooper, Joseph Hewes, and John Penn signed the document as representatives of North Carolina.

News of the Declaration of Independence travelled slowly, but wherever the people heard the news, they received it enthusiastically. In New York the soldiers of General Washington pulled down a lead statue of King George III and sent it off to

William Hooper, one of the three North Carolinians who signed the Declaration of Independence.

be melted into bullets. In some towns there were parades and various other forms of celebration. Although riders on swift horses carried the news of the Declaration, it did not reach North Carolina until July 22. The North Carolina Council of Safety at Halifax ordered that it be read to all the people of the colony. The first public reading of the Declaration of Independence in North Carolina occurred at Halifax on August 1, 1776. A large crowd gathered to hear Cornelius Harnett, President of the Council of Safety, read the document. As he finished a mighty cheer went up from the assembled people. Then, with Harnett on their shoulders, they paraded happily through the streets of the town. Within a few weeks the Declaration of Independence had been read in every town in North Carolina.

The first Provincial Congress to meet after the Declaration of Independence assembled at Halifax on November 12, 1776. A big task lay before them. Now that the colonists had declared themselves free men, they had to make provisions for governing themselves as a free people. A committee was appointed to draw up a State Constitution. The chairman of the committee was Richard Caswell, although there were some who said that Thomas Jones of Edenton did most of the work in drawing up this new outline of government. When the committee had finished its work, it was presented to the Congress. Many changes were made in the original document as the other members of the Congress debated the Constitution line by line and almost word by word.

Joseph Hewes, another of the three North Carolina signers of the Declaration of Independence.

On December 12, 1776, a Bill of Rights was voted upon and passed. The next day the Constitution received the approval of a majority of the delegates.

The Bill of Rights stated the rights of a free people. Many of those rights which previously had been denied by the King and Parliament were now listed as basic freedoms of the people of North Carolina.

The Constitution outlined a framework of government. The new government of North Carolina was to be composed of three branches: executive, legislative, and judiciary. The executive department was to be composed of a governor, a council of state, a secretary, a treasurer, and an attorney general. All these officials were to be elected by the Legislature. The primary duties of these men were to see that the laws of North Carolina were properly executed.

Laws were to be made by the legislative branch of the government—the General Assembly. This was to be a bicameral, or two-house legislature. Before any measure could become law, it had to receive a majority vote in each house of the Assembly. One of these houses, the Senate, was composed of one delegate from each county in the State. The other body was to be called the

House of Commons, with two members from every county. Those towns considered important enough also were allowed representatives in the House of Commons. There were six of these—Edenton, New Bern, Wilmington, Salisbury, Hillsboro, and Halifax— and they were termed "borough towns." Any free man, white or colored, who owned as much as fifty acres of land and had lived one month in the county and at least one year in the State could vote for senators. Any free man who had lived in the State for one year and had paid his taxes was allowed to vote for delegates to the House of Commons. Not every man could be elected to the General Assembly. A senator was required to have lived in the county for at least a year and to own at least 300 acres of land. The same length of residence was required for members of the House of Commons, but they had to own only 100 acres of land.

The judiciary was the legal division of the State and was charged with the enforcement of the laws. It included all of the judges of the State and the attorney general. The judges of the higher courts were elected by the Legislature. The judges of the lower, or county courts, were the justices of the peace. They were appointed by the governor upon the recommendation of the county representatives in the legislature. All the judges could remain in office for life so long as they behaved themselves.

Among other things, the new Constitution defined the relationship between the new State government and the Continental Congress. We had no President of the United States, nor any real national government to carry on the war—only the Continental Congress. This Congress was actually more of a combined effort by the states than an independent legislative body. No one considered it to be superior to the states, and everyone felt the state governments were more important. Yet all of the states left the operation of the war on a national scale to the Continental Congress, even though that body lacked many of the necessary powers. North Carolina's representatives to the Continental Congress were elected by the State Legislature.

Although many faults can be discovered in North Carolina's first Constitution, it must be remembered that it was drawn up by men who had little or no experience in such matters. Considering this, we can only conclude that they did a magnificent job. The Constitution they wrote served North Carolina for fifty-nine years. It was not until 1835 that the State felt it necessary to revise the original document.

George III King of England during the American Revolution.

The last official act of this Provincial Congress was to elect the first governor of North Carolina under the new Constitution. Their choice fell upon the hero of the battle of Moore's Creek Bridge, Richard Caswell.

After the adjournment of the Congress, Governor Caswell set out for New Bern. There he was to establish his residence in the fabulous Governor's Palace which had been completed by Governor William Tryon in 1770. The people at New Bern gave him a welcome that would have done credit to a king. At least thirty of the leading citizens met him six miles out of town and escorted him the remaining distance into New Bern. As the party entered the town, a mighty shout went up from the people lining the streets. From every church steeple came the rhythmic clanging of bells. Muskets cracked as soldiers fired a salute. Every vessel anchored in the harbor flew the new red and white striped Continental Flag, and every ship that carried a cannon boomed out a welcome to the new governor. The night was not so noisy, but from nearly every window in town a candle burned and flickered out a message of joy. After the conclusion of the formal celebration, the citizens of the town gathered to offer Governor Caswell their congratulations and best wishes.

It was actually several months before the State government really began functioning. On April 7, 1777, the first General Assembly of the State of North Carolina assembled in New Bern. They faced all those problems that confront any state in war time. There were soldiers to be recruited, equipped, and trained. Military supplies had to be collected and distributed to the army. There were laws to be passed. Something had to be done about the Tories. Although they had been defeated at Moore's Creek Bridge, there were still enough of them to cause trouble, if the opportunity presented itself. On the mountain frontier there was ever-present danger from Indians who held no love for the white men who had invaded their hunting grounds.

The first meeting of the General Assembly also brought to light some of the weaknesses of the State Constitution. In a time of stress and warfare a strong leader was needed, yet the Constitution had so restricted the governor of the State that it was impossible for him to exercise the proper authority. This weakness of the governor had been a reaction to the experience of the people as colonists of Great Britain. They felt that the royal governors had been invested with too much authority and they were determined to have an executive who could be controlled by the people. As a result of this attitude, Governor Caswell found himself faced by problems he did not have the power to correct.

The people themselves did not live in peace and harmony under their new Constitution. Many disagreed with the form of government that had been adopted by the new State. Others did not like the manner in which the war was being conducted. This was especially true of those who lived on the western frontier. They were trying not only to carve a living out of the wilderness, but also to protect themselves against attacks by Indians. They complained that the State was not furnishing adequate military protection against the raids of the savages. They also argued that the mountain men were not properly represented in the government of North Carolina.

The question of money was one of the greatest problems faced by the new State. North Carolina began its existence as a state with an empty treasury. Because of this scarcity of money, North Carolina could only follow the example set by the Continental Congress and the other states—they began to issue paper money. Paper money backed with only the promise to pay, rather than gold or silver, is worth little. The Continental Congress issued so much worthless paper money that we still use the expression "Not worth a Continental" to describe something worthless. North Carolina, as did the Continental Congress, found she was forced to issue more and more paper currency. The more that was printed, the less it was worth. By 1780 a man had to have at least 800 dollars in North Carolina paper money in order to buy one dollar's worth of merchandise. One newspaper carried the story of a man in New Bern who was paying 4,000 dollars a week for his board—in paper money. Money, however, was but one of many problems.

The most pressing problem facing any state at war is the military. Each year the Continental Congress called for more men to be furnished the Continental army. North Carolina and the other twelve states were each assigned quotas of men to provide for the Continental army. It was by no means an easy task to enlist the necessary number of soldiers. In fact, North Carolina and most of the other colonies were never successful in filling their quotas. Men were not eager to leave their families and farms to fight the British. Army pay was little enough to begin with, and was worth even less because of the almost valueless money. A large part of the population were Tories, who certainly wanted no part of an army fighting against that of their King. And so it went. Nevertheless, during the war North Carolina raised a total of ten regiments for the Continental Line, furnishing between 6,086 and 7,663 men to the army.

Not all of the men who carried arms in the American Revolution fought as soldiers of the Continental army. By far the greater number who served did so as members of the militia. The militia included nearly every man in the State. When an able-bodied man reached the age of sixteen, he automatically became a member of the local militia. They were poorly trained. They sometimes had only one "muster," or training session, each year, and they often were drilled by men who knew nothing of the art of warfare. Militiamen were required to furnish their own weapons, and these ranged from rickety old muskets to the deadly accurate rifles of the frontiersmen. In many instances, the law said they could not be forced to fight outside the boundaries of the State unless they consented. As a result of haphazard organizations and preparations, the men of the militia usually were considered poor soldiers. They were seldom dependable in the face of an advancing enemy. Still, it has been estimated that as many as 10,000 North Carolinians took the field as militia against the enemy during the Revolutionary War.

To the west, in the mountain country, the militia held better reputations as fighting men. They had to be in order to survive. The British had sent agents among the Indians and persuaded them to take the warpath against the white men who had settled upon their hunting grounds. In July, 1776, the Cherokees began to pour down upon the mountain settlements, massacring the inhabitants, and burning their homes. In September of that year, General Griffith Rutherford and Colonel Andrew Williamson gathered a force of 2,400 men and marched into the Cherokee country. Most of these soldiers were from North Carolina, although there were some from South Carolina and Virginia. On their swing through the Cherokee country, they set fire to crops and burned at least thirty-six Cherokee towns. The savages made one stand against the white men, but they were crushed in the brief battle and fled to the westward. Finally, on July 20, 1777, the Cherokees signed a peace treaty, in which they gave up much of the land they had claimed as their hunting grounds.

Not all the Indians gave up so easily. Dragging Canoe and several other chiefs retired westward and joined the Chickamaugas. Other Indians joined them. They later returned to harass the frontier settlements, with the result that in 1779 the states of North Carolina and Virginia sent 900 men under Colonel Evan Shelby to wipe out these warriors. They surprised the Chickamaugas, defeated them in battle and burned their villages. They did not catch Dragging Canoe, who escaped and remained a thorn in the side of the western inhabitants. There were other battles with the Cherokees, who were continually being stirred up by British agents who were furnishing them with supplies, arms, and ammunition. One war party was routed by Colonel John Sevier in an engagement in the valley of the French Broad River on December 8, 1780. Nevertheless, the Indians were never so strong as they had been before Griffith Rutherford's expedition in the summer of 1776.

Many of the soldiers of North Carolina never fought on the soil of their native state. These were the North Carolinians who had enlisted in the Continental army. Their first real military experience had been gained in 1775 when Colonel Robert Howe's regiment was sent to Virginia to aid the people of that colony in driving out their last royal governor, the Earl of Dunmore. The following year 700 North Carolinians aided in putting down a revolt by the "Scovellites," a group of back-country Tories in South Carolina. Because part of this expedition was conducted during a two-foot snowfall, it has sometimes been referred to as the "snow campaign."

They also fought in South Carolina as a sequel to the Moore's Creek Bridge campaign. When the British fleet left the Cape Fear area in the spring of 1776, they sailed to Charleston, South Carolina, to attack that city. They had expected an easy fight, but they found a large number of hard-fighting Americans defending the city, who drove off the sailors and soldiers of George III. Included in the defenders of Charleston were 1,400 soldiers from North Carolina under the command of the recently-promoted Brigadier General Robert Howe. When Major General Charles Lee, commanding the Continental army in the South, was recalled to the northern part of the country by General Washington, General Howe was promoted to this job. Shortly afterward he was promoted to major general. He remained as the commanding general in the South until December 29, 1778, when he was forced to surrender Savannah, Georgia, to a British force. Major General Robert Howe held the highest rank of any North Carolinian serving with the Continental army.

The activities of the North Carolina soldiers were not confined to the South. From 1777 to 1780, soldiers of the State served under General Washington in the North. In June, 1777, a North Carolina brigade under the command of General Francis Nash marched northward and joined the main Continental army. At that time the British army was driving toward the important City of Philadelphia. On September 11th, Washington made a stand against the enemy at Brandywine Creek. Although the Americans were driven back, the newly arrived soldiers from North Carolina won praise for their courage and gallantry in this battle.

A month later, General Washington attacked a British force in Germantown, Pennsylvania. Again, Washington lost the battle, but during the fighting the brigade under General Nash had made the greatest advance of any unit in the American army. The battle cost the North Carolinians their leader. General Nash was carried from the field suffering a mortal wound. Three days later, he died.

After Nash's death, the North Carolinians were placed under the command of General Lachlan McIntosh of Georgia. During the terrible winter of 1777-1778 they experienced the many hardships suffered by the American army at Valley Forge. During that miserable winter, they lived in crudely-built log huts, with never enough to eat; indeed it was often that they had nothing at all to cook. With their feet frequently wrapped in rags, they huddled around smoky campfires, trying to keep alive until the spring. Some died from the effects of their wounds; far more died as a result of smallpox and other diseases.

Spring finally came, and in June, 1778, the British left Philadelphia and began to march overland to New York. On a hot, sultry June day, General Washington struck them at Monmouth Court House in New Jersey. Once again he failed to defeat the enemy, but once again the North Carolina troops held firm at critical moments in the battle.

The action at Monmouth Court House was the last major battle fought by General Washington in the North. From this time on, the greatest military activity was to-be in the South—and North Carolina was destined to feel the hard stamp of war.

CHAPTER IV

DISASTER IN THE SOUTH

In 1779 the British government made a major change in its military strategy. From now on, it was decided, they would concentrate their primary efforts in the southern states. There was sound economic reasoning behind this decision. They felt they had little to gain by continuing the fight in the northern states. These states lay in the same climatic belt as England, and most of the products they grew could also be produced in England. Another disadvantage was that New England was a trading community. England's prosperity depended on her own trading efforts. As a consequence of these similar interests, the northern colonies were quite often in direct competition with the mother country.

The South, on the other hand, with its sub-tropical climate, grew products that could not be grown in England. For instance, there was the aromatic tobacco to fill the pipes and snuff-boxes of Europe. North Carolina's tall pine forests furnished the lumber, tar, and pitch needed for Great Britain's navy and merchant vessels. Rice was grown in South Carolina; the indigo grown in that same colony furnished a dye that gave European clothing a more brilliant hue. From the back country came the skins and furs that had so many uses. To put it simply, the products of the South were more valuable to England than those of the northernmost colonies. Also there were supposed to be many with loyalist sentiments in the South. These considerations led the British government to put their new plan in operation. This plan was to start as far south as Georgia, and then gradually to subdue the southern states and make them British colonies again.

In late 1778 the Georgia town of Savannah was taken. This gave the British army and naval forces a base from which they could operate. After an interval of more than a year Charleston, a most valuable seaport, was attacked. Under the command of their general, Sir Henry Clinton, the British surrounded the town. Ships in the harbor and soldiers in trenches drew an ever-tightening circle around Charleston. From late March until May, British cannon pounded the city. From time to time, British soldiers laid aside their muskets and picked up their shovels. New trenches were dug, each one a little nearer to Charleston than the last. Cavalry troops under Lieutenant Colonel Banastre Tarleton ranged the countryside, driving off American reinforcements and blocking every escape route for the defenders of the city.

General Benjamin Lincoln, commanding general of the Americans within Charleston, could see neither any hope of driving off the enemy nor any possibility of saving his army through a retreat. On May 12, 1780, the American Stars and Stripes were hauled down in surrender. General Lincoln then led his more than 5,000 crestfallen soldiers out of the town to lay down their arms. Included in these troops were 815 North Carolina Continental officers and men and approximately 600 militia from the State. This defeat, as one of the American soldiers wrote, was "a rude Shock to the Independence of America."

Francis Marion, familiarly known as the "Swamp Fox," was a guerilla leader in South Carolina.

Sir Henry Clinton sailed back to his main base in New York. As commanding general of the British army in the South, he left a short, thick-set lieutenant general. He was Charles, First Lord Cornwallis, an English nobleman who had been involved in the American War since 1776. Clinton's orders to Cornwallis were first to conquer the rest of South Carolina and Georgia, then to march into North Carolina and Virginia. Cornwallis was in no great hurry. He rested his men while he made plans for the future.

This delay on the part of the British general gave Governor Abner Nash of North Carolina an opportunity to prepare the defenses of his State. General Richard Caswell, no longer governor, but again a soldier, started to rally the militia. Small groups of daring men began to nip at the flanks of the British. In South Carolina these guerilla fighters were led by such dashing leaders as Thomas Sumter, Andrew Pickens, and the "Swamp Fox," Francis Marion. Mounted groups from North Carolina were under men equally as bold: William Richardson Davie,

William Lee Davidson, Griffith Rutherford, and Francis Locke. They rode swiftly and struck the outposts of the British suddenly and without warning. Darting quickly through the night, or making sudden daylight raids, they stung and nettled the invading redcoats.

Abner Nash was governor of North Carolina, 1780-1781.

The nearness of the British army presented another problem in North Carolina. The Tories began to grow restless and bolder. Since they had been defeated at Moore's Creek Bridge, their life had not been easy. In many instances they brought hardships upon themselves. The government of the State had first tried to win the loyalists by persuasion. When this failed, laws were passed declaring that the loyalists had to either take an oath of allegiance to North Carolina or to leave the State. Large numbers did leave, sailing either to the British strongholds in New York and Nova Scotia or to England. Some refused to leave their homes, hiding out in the forests or banding together in groups to raid and plunder the Whigs. The Whigs struck back. On both sides, houses were burned and quite often lives were lost in clashes between former friends and neighbors.

These Tories were not necessarily evil men. They did not, however, hold the same political beliefs as the Whigs. They were just as devoted to the government of George III as the Whigs were to the cause of liberty. When they heard that the army of Lord Cornwallis was just a few days march away, they began to feel that their King had not forsaken them.

The proximity of the British army also had an effect upon the Whigs. General Griffith Rutherford called out his brigade of about 800 militia. They assembled near Charlotte. The men were still coming in when, on the night of June 14th, the general received word that the Tories were gathering in Tryon County. Because Rutherford did not wish to leave Charlotte and the vicinity unguarded, he sent word to Colonel Francis Locke and Major Joseph McDowell to break up this group.

This uprising of the Tories had had its beginning in early June. A shabbily dressed man by the name of John Moore had

arrived in Lincoln County and announced that he had been appointed a lieutenant colonel in the British army. He planned to raise a company of North Carolina loyalists to fight with the redcoats of Lord Cornwallis. He designated Ramsour's Mill (near present-day Lincolnton) as a meeting place. By June 20th, 1780, nearly 1,100 men were encamped in the neighborhood of the mill, but almost 300 of them possessed no firearms. This was the group that General Rutherford had ordered Locke and McDowell to disperse.

Major Joseph McDowell was sent by General Griffith Rutherford to quell Tory outbreaks in Tryon County.

Locke had under his command between 300 and 400 men, most of them on foot. On June 20th they approached Ramsour's Mill. The Tories had pitched their camp along the crest of a long ridge. In front of them lay a long slope, free of brush, a position which gave them a good field of fire. Locke's men marched quietly through the trees at the bottom of the hill. They were not discovered until they bumped into a Tory outpost at the foot of the slope. The startled sentries fired a few scattered shots, and then fled up the hill shouting as they ran. This unexpected development threw the Tories into the wildest disorder. When Locke's few mounted troops began to gallop up the hill in pursuit of the fleeing outpost, the general confusion in the Tory camp became even greater. Many grabbed their muskets or rifles and fled. The braver men rushed forward and with their fire drove Locke's horsemen back down the hill.

By this time, Locke's foot soldiers had reached the edge of the clearing at the bottom of the hill. They took cover and began to return a steady fire. Gradually, Locke began to surround the Tories by having his men slip around the sides and to the rear of the enemy position.

Neither group was well equipped as armies go. Neither had distinctive uniforms. The Whigs wore little scraps of white paper in their hats; the Tories distinguished themselves by wearing a sprig of green leaves. Neither side had bayonets, and

when the Whigs closed in on the Tories, some used their rifles and muskets as clubs, while others fought with their fists. Moore's Tories were driven back gradually and finally they turned and ran for their lives. Behind them at least 150 of their comrades lay dead or wounded. Another fifty had been made prisoners by the Whigs. Most of the survivors scurried back to their homes, although some went with Moore to join Cornwallis in South Carolina. At least 700 of the Tories actually fought in the battle of Ramsour's Mill, but they had been defeated by Locke's little detachment of between 300 and 400 men.

Colonel Isaac Shelby's militia participated in the defeat of seasoned British troops at Musgrove Mill on the Enoree in South Carolina. Later Shelby led his troops at the Battle of King's Mountain where the British were again defeated.

This new defeat did not completely discourage the Tories. They realized that Lord Cornwallis was not too far away and that he planned to invade North Carolina. They felt that the British army, once it started marching north, would offer them protection and support in putting down the Whigs. On the other hand, the Whigs also realized this and were determined to stamp out any signs of a Tory uprising. This thought was uppermost in General Griffith Rutherford's mind when he received word that Colonel Samuel Bryan was assembling the loyalists in the forks of the Yadkin River in Rowan County. He marched towards them. Colonel Bryan, having just heard of the crushing defeat of the loyalists at Ramsour's Mill, had no intention of fighting. He pulled his troops back to the protection of the British posts in South Carolina.

Colonel William R. Davie had been sent to watch one of the British strong points near Hanging Rock, South Carolina. First he captured a supply column and then, in plain view of the garrison, he cut to pieces three companies of Tories who were returning from a raid. Shortly after this, Davie was joined by the soldiers under Colonel Thomas Sumter of South Carolina. Sumter and Davie decided to make a sudden attack on the British. Hanging Rock was defended by North Carolina Tories under Colonel Morgan Bryan and a small number of British redcoats. The Tories were routed as Davie and Sumter attacked, but the better-disciplined British soldiers stood their ground. Although the Americans soon discovered they could not dislodge the British regulars, they did capture valuable supplies in the Tory camp.

William Richardson Davie harassed British troops in North and South Carolina and aided General Gates in his retreat from Camden. Davie became governor of the State in the years after the war.

Farther to the west, the mountain men under Colonel Charles McDowell were also doing their bit to put down the enemy. McDowell crushed one party of Tories under Patrick Moore. He then dispatched Colonel Isaac Shelby and Lieutenant Colonels Elijah Clarke and James Williams to disperse an assembly of Tories camped at Musgrove's Mill on the Enoree River in South Carolina. Upon their arrival they were dismayed to discover the Tories had been reinforced by a detachment of British regulars. Shelby lured these redcoats into an ambush. When the shooting was over, the British had suffered a loss of sixty-three killed and 160 wounded and taken prisoners. In contrast, the Americans had lost only four killed and nine wounded. This little skirmish on the Enoree is significant because it was one of the few times during the American Revolution that untrained militia were able to defeat seasoned British troops.

While the local militia groups were concerned with putting down the Tories, even greater events had been taking place. These, however, were disastrous from the American point of view. After the surrender of Charleston in May, 1780, General Benjamin Lincoln had been made a prisoner-of-war. For a time there was no American general to command the Continental army in the South. As a replacement for General Lincoln, the Continental Congress had selected General Horatio Gates to command the area known as the Southern Department. Gates had won undying fame by defeating the British under General John Burgoyne at Saratoga, New York, in 1777.

General Horatio Gates won fame by defeating the British under General Burgoyne at Saratoga, New York in 1777. He was appointed to command the Department of the South in July, 1780. His glory was somewhat dimmed by his defeat at Camden, South Carolina, and he was recalled from his command in the South.

At Hillsboro, on July 25, 1780, General Gates assumed the command of the southern Continental army. At this time the army numbered around 3,000 Continental soldiers. They were joined by 1,200 North Carolina militia troops under Generals Griffith Rutherford and Richard Caswell. General Gates was impatient, and acted rashly. Soon after he had taken command of the army, he marched it southward towards the British strong point at Camden, South Carolina. His soldiers were in no condition to fight. Few of them had the necessary equipment to carry out a campaign against the enemy, and there was practically no food. As they marched along, many of the men picked and ate the green corn and peaches from the fields and orchards along the way. A large number of them became ill. Food became so scarce that some of the officers actually thickened their soup with the powder they ordinarily used to whiten their hair. It was a sick, hungry, and complaining army that marched towards Camden.

Gates decided he would approach Camden under the cover of darkness. He knew that Lord Cornwallis was aware of his arrival. By a strange coincidence, the British general decided to march out of Camden also that same night. In the blackness of a sultry August night, the armies of Generals Gates and Cornwallis stumbled into each other on a narrow stretch of land between two swamps. A few shots spattered through the night. Then both armies drew back to wait for the dawn.

As the sun came up on August 16, 1780, the battle lines of redcoats began to advance upon the Americans. Stepping across the field, they fired volley after volley, and the air rang with their shouts. They were indeed an impressive sight. Some of Gates' men stood fast, others began to fade back. Some, who had never been in battle before, turned and fled. Others followed. Their fear was contagious, and soon most of the American army was hastening from the field. A few brave men stood firm, but they were not enough to stem the onrushing red uniforms. They were crushed as the British battle lines rolled over them.

With his frightened men streaming from the battlefield, General Gates joined them in retreat, leaving nearly 800 dead Americans and nearly 1,000 more who had been captured by the British. The enemy had captured most of General Gates' equipment, arms, and ammunition. Nearly one-half of those killed in the battle of Camden were North Carolinians. General Griffith Rutherford was listed among the captured officers.

Gates stopped first in Charlotte. He decided that this was not the place to attempt a reorganization of his army and rode on. In three days of hard riding he covered the 180 miles from Camden in South Carolina to Hillsboro in North Carolina. At Hillsboro he halted and began slowly to rebuild an army out of the beaten survivors of the battle of Camden.

Victorious, Lord Cornwallis rested in Camden. His plans were not yet complete for an invasion of North Carolina. On September 8, he moved his army up to a place called the Waxhaws and encamped, hoping that the Tories of the neighborhood would come in and enlist in his army. His stay there was not peaceful. Colonel William R. Davie, with 150 hard-riding men, swooped down upon an outpost of 300 British soldiers at Wahab's Plantation. The British were so surprised that they allowed Davie to capture ninety-three of their horses. By the time they recovered, Davie and his men had disappeared into the forest.

Little skirmishes such as these did not prevent Lord Cornwallis from making his plans. In his invasion of North Carolina, Hillsboro, the most important town in what was then the western part of the State, was his first goal. He hoped he would be able to drive straight up through the center of the State, by way of Charlotte, Salisbury, Salem, and Guilford Court House, and then on to Hillsboro. Tories were expected to rise and join his army as they marched through. At Hillsboro he planned to secure both recruits and supplies for his army, for, according to Governor Martin, that town was supposed to be a regular hotbed of loyalists. On paper, this campaign appeared easy, but the British general was too good a soldier to take things for granted.

Because Cornwallis feared the rough and tumble frontiersmen who lived in the mountains to the west, he sent Major Patrick Ferguson to try to keep them under control. To the east, the Cape Fear River furnished a waterway on which supplies could be brought as far inland as Cross Creek. Wilmington, at the mouth of the river, must be kept under British control. A detachment under Major James Craig was sent to protect that town.

It was only after his careful plans were completed that Lord Cornwallis issued marching orders to his army. As the long column moved slowly along, the partisan bands of Marion and Sumter pecked away at their flanks. They did little harm, but they did keep the British in a constant state of alarm. On September 28, followed by their long line of creaking supply wagons, Lord Cornwallis's army marched into Charlotte. Even then, Colonel Davie, with a small group of mounted men forced the entire British army to halt for several minutes on the outskirts of the town.

Charlotte, named for the queen of George III, was but a small village in 1780. The courthouse and a few small wooden structures made up the entire town. There was one advantage—a number of grist mills in the area could be used to grind grain into the flour needed to feed the army.

Accompanying the army was a familiar figure, Governor Josiah Martin. He was still as confident as ever that Cornwallis would have to do little more than march his men through the State, and North Carolina would again become a royal colony. The governor's first move was to issue a proclamation and dispatch riders to distribute it throughout the State. In this document, he confidently declared that the victorious British army was now in control of North Carolina, and once again the State was under royal rule. He could not have made a more serious error.

Although Josiah Martin had served four years as governor of North Carolina, he had never really known its people, especially those of Mecklenburg and Rowan counties. They made life miserable for the British soldiers. Nervous British sentries fired at the smallest sound. Foraging parties, sent out to collect food, were ambushed and attacked by small groups of angry patriots. Detachments of troops sent to guard the grist mill were harassed almost constantly. Snipers hid in the trees and picked off careless British soldiers. Bright red coats made good targets for men who were accustomed to aiming at the eye of a squirrel.

Lord Cornwallis had hoped that Charlotte and the surrounding countryside would prove a land of plenty. It wasn't. Instead, he found he had stirred up a hornet's nest and was soon writing Sir Henry Clinton that the people of Mecklenburg and Rowan counties were "more hostile to England than any in America."

Then, on October 12, a messenger, riding out of the west, splashed through the muddy streets of Charlotte. The news he bore knocked all British plans into a cocked hat. So distressing was his information, that the British general gave orders to his troops to pack and move back into South Carolina.

CHAPTER V

THE "BULL DOG" ON THE MOUNTAIN

The news which had led Lord Cornwallis to make such a
sudden change in his plans concerned Major Patrick Ferguson.
Ferguson was one of the most promising young officers in the
British army. He had been a soldier since he was fifteen years
old, and had fought in the American War for nearly five years.
He had invented a breech-loading rifle, and was recognized
generally as one of the best marksmen in all England. Patrick
Ferguson proved himself to be such a stubborn fighter that his
fellow officers had nicknamed him the "Bull Dog." Since he had
been in the South, Cornwallis had assigned him the task of
recruiting the Tories and organizing them into trained fighting
units.

In Lord Cornwallis's master plan for the invasion of North
Carolina and Virginia, Ferguson had been assigned the important task of protecting the left flank of the British army.
Recently, he had been pursuing small groups of rebels through
the mountains and enlisting Tories to serve in the army of the
King. He had advanced as far westward as Gilbert Town (near
present-day Rutherfordton). There he had halted. From this
small mountain settlement he sent word to "Over the Mountain
Men," that if they did not lay down their arms he would "march
his army over the mountains, hang their leaders, and lay their
country waste with fire and sword."

For all of his skill and bravery as a soldier, this was a foolish
move by Patrick Ferguson. No one, especially a person whom
they considered to be an enemy, spoke to the mountain men in
such language. It was not long before spies brought word to
Ferguson that the mountain men were assembling to march
against him. The scouts estimated that rebels outnumbered
Ferguson's group by as much as three to one. Although Major
Ferguson was worried by this report, he had no intention of
showing his concern. He sent out a call to all persons who remained loyal to the King to bring their guns to camp and be
ready to fight the "mongrels of the back-country." He next dispatched a messenger to Charlotte, asking for help from Lord
Cornwallis. Without waiting for an answer from the British

The Battle of King's Mountain, October 7, 1780, where the British were defeated and suffered severe losses.

general, Ferguson struck his tents and hastened towards Charlotte and the protection of the British army.

The mountain patriots assembled at Sycamore Flats on the Watauga River. There were 240 men from Sullivan County (now in Tennessee) under Colonel Isaac Shelby; 160 men came from Burke and Rutherford counties under the command of Colonel Charles McDowell; and Colonel John Sevier led 240 men from Washington County (now in Tennessee). They were joined by 400 men under Colonel William Campbell who had marched down from Washington County, Virginia. Once they had all assembled, this fast-growing little army began its march across the mountains, sometimes wading through ankle-deep snow. Benjamin Cleveland, with 350 men from Wilkes and Surry counties joined them at Quaker Meadows on the Catawba River (near Morganton).

At Gilbert Town they learned that Ferguson had halted his retreat towards Charlotte and was preparing to make a stand at King's Mountain, near the North Carolina-South Carolina border. The mountain men hurried towards that spot. Colonel John Williams with another 400 men joined them at a place called the Cowpens in South Carolina. A steady rain began to fall. All that day and night they marched through the downpour towards their enemy on King's Mountain. On Saturday morning, October 7, 1780, they arrived at the foot of the mountain.

King's Mountain is not very high as mountains go. It is almost flat at the summit, but its slopes are steep, rocky, and covered with trees and brush. On top, where the ground is level, Ferguson had placed his 1,100 men. So sure was he of the strength of this position that he boasted that "he was on King's Mountain, and that he was king of that mountain. . . ." Because of the thick growth of underbrush, he could not see the mountain men as they approached through the still-dripping trees.

At the foot of King's Mountain, in the army of about 1,800, men were dismounting from their horses and checking their rifles. Some placed white scraps of paper in their hats so they could be recognized. Their officers spoke encouraging words, reminding them to act bravely in the face of enemy fire. They spread out and surrounded the mountain. Then, as the first rifle spat its deadly message, the mountain men gave a war whoop and began to scramble up the steep slopes. Now and then they halted long enough to take refuge behind a tree and squeeze off a shot at the enemy.

The British and the Tories on top of the mountain were stunned momentarily by this sudden and unexpected attack. Ferguson, wearing a plaid hunting shirt to protect his uniform from the rain, signaled his men into position with the little silver whistle he wore around his neck. Throughout the battle the shrill shriek of the whistle could be heard above the rattle of the musketry as Ferguson maneuvered his men from one position to another. The plaid shirt, the silver whistle, and the sword hanging by his side made the British major a natural target for the sharpshooters among the Americans.

On came the rebels. Some slipped down the wet slope as they lost their footing; others grabbed a convenient bush in order to pull themselves along. Suddenly, the silver whistle was heard no more. Several rifle balls, at almost the same instant, had knocked Ferguson from his horse. The "Bull Dog" was dead. His second-in-command ordered the white flag of surrender. The firing stopped. Colonel Isaac Shelby shouted for Ferguson's men to throw down their arms. They did. The battle was over.

On the side of the mountain where he had died, Ferguson was buried under a pile of rocks. One hundred and fifty seven of his men had been killed, 163 wounded, and 698 had been taken prisoner by the rebels. Soon after the battle, most of the mountain men returned to their homes. Some stayed to guard the prisoners when they were marched to Hillsboro to be turned over to General Gates.

Ferguson's defeat at King's Mountain was responsible for the sudden change in the plans of Cornwallis. With Ferguson out of the way, he was afraid that the rebels from the mountain regions would attack the British outposts in South Carolina, if the army marched into North Carolina. On October 14, he issued marching orders to his troops. In the steady, cold, October rain his red-coats sloshed their way through the mud on the return to South Carolina. Many of the soldiers, including Lord Cornwallis, became sick. The laboring and lumbering column was harassed almost continually by little groups under Colonels Davie and Davidson. Fifteen days after they left Charlotte, a bedraggled British army straggled into Winnsboro, South Carolina. Almost immediately, Cornwallis wrote Sir Henry Clinton requesting reinforcements—enough men to allow him to make another effort.

The first invasion of North Carolina had ended in dismal failure.

Up in Hillsboro, General Gates received the news that Cornwallis had retreated from Chariotte. He immediately marched his little army of about 1,000 men to that place. He was not to remain there very long. Ever since he had been so disastrously defeated in the battle of Camden, many people had demanded his removal as commander of the southern army. So persistent were these demands that the Continental Congress ordered General Washington to appoint a general to succeed General Gates.

On December 5, 1780, a stockily-built, stern-faced, major general rode into Charlotte and took over the command of the army from Horatio Gates. This was Nathanael Greene, the "fighting Quaker." Greene, a Rhode Islander, had at one time been a member of the Quaker Church. Before the war he had worked with his father making iron anchors for ships. He had no military experience and an injured knee gave him a permanent limp; yet, despite these handicaps he had become a major general in the Continental army. Nathanael Greene had fought the British since the siege of Boston in 1775, and at one time had served as Quartermaster General. This was the man chosen by General Washington to replace General Gates.

There were, in addition to General Greene, two other newcomers to the southern army. Both were destined to play an important role in the months ahead and both were from Virginia. One was the gigantic brigadier general, Daniel Morgan. Twenty years earlier, during the French and Indian War, a British officer had ordered Morgan whipped for some infraction of the rules. The scars left by the lash were still visible on his back. He hated the sight of any soldier in a red coat. Since the very beginning of the Revolution he had fought the British from Canada to South Carolina. The days of exposure were beginning to tell on the magnificent body that held the soul of Daniel Morgan. Rheumatism now made every step he took a painful effort, but not even suffering could dim the fighting spirit of this man from the frontiers of Virginia.

The other Virginian was a cocky little cavalry leader, Lieutenant Colonel Henry Lee. To the army he was known as "Light Horse Harry." The unit he commanded was known as the American Legion, a group of specially selected men who rode swift horses and fought like demons. In their white leather breeches, green jackets, and plumed leather helmets, they were probably the best-dressed outfit in the American army. Because of the speed with which they moved, the American Legion was particularly valuable in observing the movements of the enemy.

Soon after assuming command of the army, General Nathanael Greene not only made a thorough inspection of his soldiers, but also had a careful survey made of the country near Charlotte. He decided that there was not enough food in the vicinity to feed his army. Therefore he ordered the major portion of his army to take up a position on the Pee Dee River in South Carolina (the Yadkin River becomes the Pee Dee before reaching South Carolina). A smaller group of around 1,000 men, which included some 300 North Carolina troops, was placed under the command of General Morgan.

Daniel Morgan was a native of Virginia, a brigadier general and a veteran of the French and Indian War. He defeated the British at Cowpens.

These, Greene ordered into northwest South Carolina, near the town and British post, of Ninety Six. This splitting of the army not only provided Greene and Morgan with a better opportunity to secure provisions for their men, but enabled them to observe more closely the movements of the British. When, and if, Lord Cornwallis did start a drive northward into North Carolina and Virginia, he would have to march between these two American groups. Greene and Morgan could then close in and hammer at his flanks.

On the other hand, Lord Cornwallis was no fool. He had no intention of allowing himself to be caught in a trap of this nature.

Because Morgan's group was the smaller of the two and its position was nearer to the British army, the British general decided to eliminate it. For this task he selected the hard-riding British Legion of Lieutenant Colonel Banastre Tarleton. Of all the officers in the British army, Tarleton was the most hated by the Americans in the South. He had roamed up and down South Carolina, burning houses, plundering homes, and slaughtering cattle. Because of his ruthlessness, both on and off the battlefield, he was known as "Bloody" Tarleton. He was delighted when he received the assignment to wipe out Morgan. Almost immediately he started marching for the American position.

Lieutenant Colonel Henry Lee, "Light Horse Harry," of Virginia, was in command of a unit known as the American Legion, a fast-moving troop, invaluable in scouting service.

Morgan retreated. Through the fields and forests he fled, sometimes just ahead of the oncoming British. When he reached a place called Hannah's Cowpens on the Broad River, he halted his men and made ready for the battle. There, in the area usually used by grazing cattle, he placed his soldiers in three battle lines. With their backs to the river, there was no chance to retreat; his men had to stand and fight. When the rash Tarleton came on the scene, he immediately charged Morgan's position. He was, however, sent reeling back in a smashing and unexpected defeat. Almost the entire British Legion was taken prisoner. The Americans captured much booty, including valuable equipment, arms, and ammunition. Tarleton himself was able to escape only because he rode a fast horse. Accompanied by just a few of his men, he dashed madly to the protection of Cornwallis's camp.

Daniel Morgan had won an outstanding victory over one of the crack units in the British army. Nevertheless, he knew full well that he would not have time for the celebration such a feat deserved. Cornwallis would never allow such a humiliating blow to British military prowess to go unpunished. The whole British army would soon be down upon the victorious Americans. Morgan was too smart to allow this to happen. He left a small detachment to bury the dead and care for the wounded. A messenger was sent to carry the news to General Greene. On the same day as the battle, January 17, 1781, and almost before his men had an opportunity to rest after the battle, Morgan started them marching northwards toward North Carolina.

When Tarleton dashed into Cornwallis's camp, the British general reacted to the news of the battle of Cowpens just as

Morgan had anticipated. He made preparations straightway for the pursuit of Morgan. The long line of redcoated soldiers marched slowly and gained little on Morgan's men. The heavily loaded baggage wagons mired down in swollen streams and muddy roads. At the end of one week, on January 25th, his army had crept only as far as Ramsour's Mill. There, encamped on the same hillside where the Whigs and the Tories had fought so desperately the previous June 20th, Lord Cornwallis made a major decision. To lighten his load, he decided to burn all of his wagons

Lieutenant Colonel Banastre Tarleton, commanding British cavalry troops, called "Bloody" Tarleton for his outrages against civilians and soldiers in the Revolution. This picture is from a portrait by Sir Joshua Reynolds, painted for Tarleton's mother in 1782.

and excess baggage. For two days a great bonfire blazed as wagons, extra uniforms, shoes, tents, and other equipment were consumed by the flames. Only enough wagons to transport the ammunition, the sick, and the wounded, were saved from destruction. On January 28th, the pursuit of Morgan was resumed.

In the meantime Morgan's messenger had reached the camp of General Greene on the Pee Dee. After a brief celebration of the victory at the Cowpens, Greene moved fast. Marching orders were issued. The army of the Pee Dee was placed under the command of General Isaac Huger of South Carolina. They were told to march northward and join Morgan's troops at Guilford Court House in North Carolina. Then, with only a sergeant's guard as an escort, Greene rode swiftly across country to join Morgan.

Shortly after two o'clock in the afternoon of January 31st, General Greene arrived at Beatty's Ford on the Catawba River. Morgan was waiting for him, although his soldiers had been sent on to Salisbury. There were no bridges across the river, and the only possible way for Cornwallis to cross the Catawba was to ford the stream. Morgan's men had already felled a number of trees in most of the fords to make this crossing more difficult.

As Greene and Morgan talked, General William Lee Davidson rode up. Davidson was in command of the militia in this area, and if he could not prevent the British from crossing the Catawba, he was to slow their pursuit. Even as the three generals sat on a log discussing their next move, a group of redcoats appeared on the opposite shore. An officer, whom they believed to be Lord Cornwallis, peered across the river through a spy glass. As he looked, Greene and Morgan finished their discussion and rode off towards Salisbury.

General Davidson then divided his militia between the two fords that the British were most likely to use—Beatty's and Cowan's. Greene had warned Davidson that Cornwallis possibly would try to throw the Americans off balance by making a big show at one ford and then crossing at another. This was exactly what Cornwallis had planned. Several pieces of artillery, all of the wagons, and a small number of troops were dispatched to Beatty's Ford. While they made noisy preparations to cross the river, the main body of the army marched to Cowan's Ford, some four miles down the river. They had started at one o'clock in the morning, and much of their time was lost stumbling along dark and unfamiliar roads. It was near daybreak when they first saw the twinkling campfires of the North Carolina militia guarding the opposite shore.

The militia were sleeping soundly, confident that their sentries would warn them in plenty of time should the British attempt a crossing at this point. It was a foggy morning, and not yet light enough to see the redcoats enter the muddy waters. The waters were swift, and the sentries soon heard the splashing of the water as the British struggled along, trying to maintain their footing on the slippery bottom. Although the American sentries were not able to see the enemy, they fired several shots at the sounds. Awakened by the shots, the militia rushed to the river bank and took up positions behind the trees.

Out in the river, the British were experiencing rough going. They had roped themselves together to prevent being swept away by the current, but some were still pulled beneath the surface. Two of Cornwallis's generals received an unexpected ducking as their horses lost their footing and rolled over. Governor Martin had his fine hat swept down the stream. Now there were the whining musket balls that came singing into their midst. Undaunted, the British struggled on.

The advance units leading the redcoats reached the shore. They scrambled up the muddy bank, loading their muskets and fixing their bayonets as they formed a battle line. They fired volley after volley to protect their dripping comrades as they came up out of the river. The militia, knowing they would soon be outnumbered, began to drift towards the rear. General Davidson tried to rally them. He was just putting his foot into the stirrup to mount his horse, when a musket ball slammed into his chest. Their commanding officer dead, the militia began to run. Soon there was no opposition and the enemy finished their crossing unmolested.

Cornwallis sent out his cavalry under Tarleton to scour the countryside and prevent the militia from reassembling. Tarleton found a large group of the North Carolinians assembling at a place called Torrence's Tavern. Before the North Carolinians could form a battle line, Tarleton and his men were upon them, swinging their sabers and firing pistols at close range. The militia scattered. The British army again took up the pursuit of Morgan's men.

They were hard on the heels of the Americans. At times they were so close that Greene's rear guard could look back and see the rolling clouds of smoke as the enemy fired some farmhouse along the way. On they came, through Salisbury, across the Yadkin River, and finally, on February 6th, Greene's cold, wet, and hungry men filed into the area around Guilford Court House. Three days later, the army of the Pee Dee marched in, many of them without shoes, leaving bloody footprints as their feet were torn and cut by the frozen ground.

Greene hoped that he would be able to make a stand at Guilford, but he soon felt that this was hopeless. He began a dash for the Dan River which flowed along the boundary between North Carolina and Virginia. Now he was without Morgan. The giant Virginian was so crippled by arthritis and rheumatism that he was forced to leave the army.

The retreat from Guilford to the Dan River was almost like a game of hare and hounds. There were numerous little skirmishes between the rear guard of Greene and the advance guard of Cornwallis. Although these little clashes seldom amounted to much, every time one occurred, there was no way for Cornwallis to know whether it was a small group, or Greene's entire army. And during every clash, the British would deploy in battle formation. This slowed the British and earned precious hours for the Americans.

Late in the afternoon of February 14th, the last of Greene's rear guard began to cross the Dan at a place called Boyd's Ferry. They were rowed across in boats, their weary horses swimming along behind. They were barely across when the redcoats appeared on the opposite shore. Their packs had been discarded so that they might make better time, and in the last twenty-four hours they had marched forty miles. This was almost phenomenal marching time. It did them little good. The British general had lost the race to the Dan.

Chapter VI

THE BATTLE OF GUILFORD COURT HOUSE

Greene's retreat did not end with his crossing of the Dan River. He led his footsore army as far north as Halifax Court House in Virginia. There he allowed them to rest while supplies were collected and additional troops enlisted. Greene spent much of his time at his writing desk. Letters were sent to Governor Abner Nash of North Carolina, Governor Thomas Jefferson of Virginia, and General Washington. He begged them to reinforce his little army with troops, equipment, and supplies. Letters also went to other important political figures, including Patrick Henry, asking them to exercise their influence to encourage enlistments in the army.

Meanwhile, Cornwallis had given up the chase. His army was dangerously low on supplies and his men were tired. He marched them towards Hillsboro. In that town he not only planned to gather food and forage, but also to persuade the Tories of that region to enlist under his command. On February 20, 1781, Lord Cornwallis and his army marched jauntily into Hillsboro. The next day, to the ceremonial booming of a twenty-one gun salute by the artillery, the Royal Standard (the flag of the King) was raised. Cornwallis issued a proclamation, declaring that he had come to rescue the loyal subjects of North Carolina "from the cruel tyranny under which they have groaned for several years." All loyalists were urged to come into Hillsboro and join the army of George III. Governor Josiah Martin also busied himself, trying to re-establish his position as the royal governor of North Carolina.

A number of Tories did ride into Hillsboro, but after looking things over, few expressed a desire to join the British army. Many of them felt that Cornwallis's army was too small to fight Greene's army and protect their families at the same time. Others argued that the British general had allowed Greene to outwit him. Others felt that the British Government had treated them rather shabbily since the beginning of the war.

The British soldiers were restless. As a means of keeping them out of mischief, and to prevent them from plundering the very people they were supposed to protect, Lord Cornwallis put them to work paving the streets of the town with cobblestones.

In the forests on the outskirts of Hillsboro, little groups of patriots concealed themselves. When a redcoat wandered too far from his comrades, he was picked off by sharpshooters. Orders had to be issued forbidding them to leave the town. Detachments sent to grind corn in the neighborhood mills were sometimes cut to pieces by fast-riding groups similar to that led by Captain Joseph Graham.

General Greene also sent two units back across the Dan to observe the movements of the enemy. These were the Legion of Light Horse Harry Lee and another group under the command of Andrew Pickens of South Carolina. By accident, they stumbled into a group of Tories, under Doctor John Pyle, marching to Hillsboro to join Cornwallis. Lee's Legion were uniformed in green jackets similar to those worn by the British Legion of Banastre Tarleton, and Pyle and his men thought that they were the British group. They were small fry so far as Lee was concerned. He was after bigger game. Word had come that Tarleton himself was camped not too far away, and Lee was on the trail of the British cavalry leader, for whom he had planned a surprise attack. When he met Pyle's Tories, he planned to allow them to think that he was Tarleton and march right on past them.

Lee had made this decision on the spur of the moment and had no time to inform his men of the plan. The Tories stepped to the side of the road to allow the Legion to pass. Some of the men near the end of the column recognized the sprigs of green in the hats of the men by the roadside. Tories! Swords were snatched from their scabbards as they wheeled towards the enemy. The stunned Tories could not believe their eyes! Tarleton's men attacking friends? They began to cry out, "Hurrah for King George," and "I am a friend to his Majesty." The only answer was the charging horses. Flashing cavalry sabers cut them down. A few fired a wild shot or two, but then they joined their comrades scampering through the trees. Behind them they left ninety of their number dead, and a number of those who escaped later died of their wounds. Lee and Pickens suffered the loss of one horse hit by a stray bullet.

This little battle ruined any chance Lee had of surprising Tarleton. The Colonel of the British Legion was warned and he quickly scurried back to Hillsboro and the protection of Lord Cornwallis's army.

Colonel Otho H. Williams of Maryland was given command of a smaller unit of General Nathanael Greene's army when the latter returned to North Carolina in February, 1781. The Maryland troops were outstanding in gallantry at the Battle of Guilford Court House.

Two weeks had now passed since Greene had crossed into Virginia. Up at Halifax Court House, he had received some supplies and new troops were coming in. Still more recruits were on the march to join him. An army is no good when it hides from the enemy, so on February 23, 1781, the American army recrossed the Dan River back into North Carolina.

Three days later Cornwallis pulled out of Hillsboro. All the food in the neighborhood had been consumed by hungry British mouths. The next camp was on Alamance Creek, between the Deep and Haw rivers. The supply situation was corrected by this march. Here the British general waited for Greene's next move.

Greene kept his men constantly on the move, feeding them off the land, and never camping two nights in the same place. He divided his army, placing the smaller number under the command of Colonel Otho Williams of Maryland. These were ordered to take a position between the main American army and the British. There was almost constant skirmishing.

Cornwallis was determined to force a showdown with Greene. Around 5:30 in the morning of March 6th, he marched his army out into the fog, hoping to surprise his enemy. Marching swiftly, they were within two miles of Williams's camp before they were discovered. The Americans immediately broke camp and began a fast retreat towards Greene's army. At Wetzell's Mill they splashed across the Reedy Fork Creek. Here Williams halted his soldiers and stationed them on the far side. As the redcoats waded into the water they were met with blistering fire. They staggered back. British artillery was brought up to furnish a covering fire for the crossing. Williams, now badly outnumbered, continued his retreat. The British turned back only after they had pursued him for another five miles.

Despite the increased number of men in his army, General Greene was still cautious. Most of his men were untrained and had never smelled the smoke of battle. Cornwallis's troops were battle-tested veterans. Greene moved his men about, as if he were playing a giant game of chess with his opponent. On March 10th, at the High Rock Ford on Haw River, a large number of reinforcements came in. Now, he felt, his army was strong enough to do battle.

In February, on his retreat through North Carolina, Guilford Court House had appealed to Greene as a battleground. Now he began to work his way back towards that site. From High Rock Ford he marched to Speedwell Iron Works on Troublesome Creek (near present-day Reidsville). Here he left most of his baggage and moved to Guilford Court House.

Cornwallis was also on the move. From Alamance Creek his army marched to South Buffalo Creek (present site of Greensboro). From here he moved to the Quaker Meeting House at New Garden, between the forks of the Deep River. On March 14th, scouts brought him word that Greene was camped at Guilford Court House. He planned a little surprise for the Americans. At daybreak, on the morning of March 15, 1781, the red column moved towards Guilford.

Spies kept Greene informed of every movement of the enemy. Lee and his Legion were ordered out to observe and harass the British. Scouting in front of Cornwallis's troops was Banastre Tarleton and his Legion. Skilfully, Lee led Tarleton into an ambush. A sharp skirmish followed. Fresh troops were sent up to aid the British. Lee galloped back to the courthouse with the news of the approach of the enemy.

Greene had already prepared a warm reception. His army numbered about 4,000 men, much larger than the 2,253 commanded by Cornwallis. But the Britishers were well-trained professional soldiers whose eyes had often smarted from burnt powder. On the other hand, many of Greene's men belonged to the militia, and no one could predict the behavior of these men under the strain of battle.

The battleground selected by the American general was a long, sloping, and almost-steep hill. At the bottom of the slope a creek skipped along between its banks. The main highway from Hillsboro to Salisbury ran through the middle of the large open area selected as the battlefield. Here Greene placed his troops in three battle lines.

About half-way down the slope was a rail fence. Here were stationed the North Carolina militia under Generals John Butler and Thomas Eaton. Behind them, on the highway, were placed two of Greene's four cannon. Farther up the slope there was another line composed of General Lawson's Virginia militia. These, however, were better soldiers than the average militia men, for most of them had been in battle before. The third line was at the crest of the hill. This was made up of the Continental troops, the best fighting men in the American army. Here were placed the remaining two cannon, and on the flanks were stationed the cavalry units of Colonels Lee and William Washington.

When the troops were in position, General Greene rode among them, talking with them and trying to keep their spirits up. He promised the North Carolina militia in the front line that if they would only fire two volleys at the British, they would be free to leave the field. He told the Virginians to allow the North Carolinians to come through their ranks when they began to retreat. Then the general rode back to the rear line and there sat resting on his horse, awaiting the arrival of the enemy.

About one-thirty in the afternoon the British came into view. Almost immediately the American cannon began to thunder out a deadly welcome. Cornwallis brought up his own artillery and soon the thump of British cannon answered. Redcoats spread out in a battle line. Now and then one of the soldiers would topple out of the ranks as an American sharpshooter caught him in his sights. The long red line began to move across the muddy field towards the first American position.

As the British approached the rail fence, it suddenly seemed to blossom in a blaze of fire. Men fell. The red line wavered for a moment, then resumed its steady advance. Forty yards away the ugly muzzles of rifle and musket barrels could be seen resting on the rails. For a moment, the British soldiers appeared to falter, but they were rallied quickly by their officers. They raised their muskets to their shoulders and fired a volley. Then, with a shout, they hurled themselves in a bayonet charge at the men behind the rail fence.

The North Carolina militia men behind the rail fence were not cowards, but neither were they supermen. Few, if any, had ever been in battle before. It is doubtful that very many had bayonets for their own arms with which they could meet the bayonet charge of the British. When they saw the line of cold steel bearing down upon them, they broke. Some threw away their guns as they fled, others withdrew more slowly, firing a few fleeting shots at the enemy as they retreated. Generals Butler and Eaton tried to rally their troops, but soon discovered they were shouting at a whirlwind. The second line of the Virginia militia opened ranks and allowed the men of the first line to storm through.

The British line resumed a steady advance. Again the British were met by a blast of fire from the second line. Again they faltered, but as before they reformed and pushed on. General Lawson, commanding the Virginians, was wounded and carried from the field. His men began a slow orderly retreat. A British charge quickened their pace. Leading the charge was Lord Cornwallis himself. His horse was killed. He quickly caught another and remounted.

After the dispersal of the second line, the British advanced upon Greene's third and last battle line. For the most part, they were seasoned Continental soldiers, except for the Second Maryland Regiment, which was made up of raw recruits. When these new soldiers, fresh to the noise of battle, saw the British soldiers with bayonets ready, and quick-stepping across the field, they broke into a disorderly retreat as the North Carolinians had done. The veteran First Maryland Regiment, however, stood firm. Their concentrated and well-aimed fire forced the British to take shelter in a ravine. General Greene rode along behind his soldiers, shouting words of encouragement to keep up their spirits.

Reinforcements to bolster the British line were brought up. Once more they charged, and again they were met by a galling fire. As soon as they had delivered this volley, the First Maryland charged with the bayonet. At the same instant, Colonel William Washington was ordered to make a cavalry charge. The sudden volley, the unexpected bayonet charge, the appearance of Washington's saber-swinging dragoons, threw the redcoats into a panic. They reeled back under this onslaught. Lord Cornwallis rode recklessly among his men in an attempt to rally them. They continued to fall back. With this, the British general galloped back to his cannon and ordered them to fire a round of grape shot into the midst of Washington's men. It was pointed out that British soldiers were in the line of fire between the cannon and the Americans. Nevertheless, Cornwallis repeated his order to fire. The answering roar of the cannon sent grape shot ripping across the field. British soldiers were killed at the same time as the Americans with whom they were fighting. The round of grape shot did halt the British retreat. Cornwallis brought up fresh troops. Greene's men began to fall back.

The redcoats reformed and again resumed their methodical advance. The horses pulling General Greene's artillery were killed, and all four American cannon were captured. The British battle line now stretched out longer than that of the Americans, which meant that Greene's men could be surrounded. And now there were no cannon to break the red battle line. Nathanael Greene, to avoid the encirclement of his army, gave orders for a retreat.

It was around three-thirty in the chill, cloudy afternoon of March 15th when the battle-weary Americans withdrew from Guilford Court House. Early the next morning they trudged into their camp at Speedwell Iron Works on Troublesome Creek, wet, cold, hungry, and tired. There was no time to rest. Expecting another attack from Cornwallis, Greene gave orders to dig in. In the midst of a steady downpour of rain, the soldiers laid down their firearms and began to throw up mud into earthworks.

Back at the battleground, Lord Cornwallis was in no mood to pursue Greene. Darkness came on fast, and rain had begun to fall. The British soldiers had no opportunity to rest, for their tents had been left back at New Garden Meeting House. For the next two days, in an almost continuous downpour of rain, they remained on the battlefield, caring for the wounded and burying the dead. American wounds were dressed as well as those of the British.

Because he had forced General Greene to leave the field, Lord Cornwallis claimed the battle of Guilford Court House as a British victory. On the other hand, he had lost some of his best troops in the engagement. In fact, so many redcoats had felt the bitter sting of American lead, that Cornwallis did not dare seek another battle with Greene. The battle had been the most violent of his military career, and he was supposed to have later said, "I never saw such fighting since God made me. The Americans fought like demons." When his claim of victory reached

England his casualty figures made such a boast seem empty. The British politician, Charles James Fox, exclaimed, "Another such victory would destroy the British Army." Crusty old Horace Walpole rumbled, "Lord Cornwallis has conquered his troops out of shoes and provisions, and himself out of troops."

On Sunday, March 18th, the British army marched away from Guilford. Its destination was to the east. Major James Craig had captured Wilmington, and there were supposed to be supplies in that city, or possibly even at Cross Creek. Before he left Guilford, Cornwallis had issued a proclamation, boasting of his victory, and calling upon all loyal persons to join his army. An offer was also made to pardon all rebels if they would only lay down their arms and give their word to fight no more. This was a hollow gesture, for Cornwallis marched away on the very day he issued the proclamation. A number of his more seriously wounded men were left at New Garden Meeting House, to be cared for by the gentle Quakers of that community.

The march was at a leisurely pace. Every grist mill along the way was used to grind grain for the flour needed to feed the soldiers. From Bell's Mill in Guilford to Dixon's Mill in Chatham County they marched. It was at Ramsey's Mill on the Deep River that Greene finally caught up with the British army.

When Greene first heard of Cornwallis's march towards the coast, he hurriedly decamped from the Ironworks. A number of the American wounded, who were too weak to travel swiftly, were left at Guilford Court House in care of the Quakers in that area. His men marched fast. Lee's Legion was sent out ahead of the army, and soon it was harassing the edges of the marching British column. A number of prisoners were taken.

At Ramsey's Mill (now Lockville), Lee skirmished briefly with a portion of Cornwallis's army, and prevented them from destroying the bridge over the river. This kept the road for pursuit open. Cornwallis quickened his pace. The hare was now chasing the hounds. General Greene, upon his arrival at Ramsey's Mill, decided to call off the pursuit. The enlistment time of many of his soldiers would soon expire and they were anxious to return to their homes. Their departure would weaken the American army too much to risk another battle with the British. For several days they rested, until the order was given to return to South Carolina. Greene hoped to increase the size of his force, attack the British posts in that state and force Cornwallis to return to the southward. There was one other consideration in

Greene's decision. With two armies marching back and forth across North Carolina, the land had been so ravaged that there was not enough food or supplies even for one group. On April 6,

Cornwallis's Headquarters. After leaving Guilford Court House, he reached Wilmington, April, 1781. There he established his headquarters in one of the finer houses.

Lord Cornwallis had hoped to find the answers to some of his supply problems in Cross Creek. Major Craig was supposed to send supplies from Wilmington up the Cape Fear River to this town. Sharp-shooting Whigs stationed on the high banks along the narrow stretches of the river, however, had made it impossible for British supply boats to navigate the stream. The loyalists of the community still remembered Moore's Creek Bridge and were not too enthusiastic about enlisting or furnishing supplies for the British army. Food was scarce in Cross Creek, and there was an outbreak of smallpox in the community, so Lord Cornwallis on April first, gave orders for the march to Wilmington.

It was a tired, dirty, and footsore army that straggled along the sandy roads of the coastal plains. Rain and sun had faded bright red coats to a pale pink. Nearly every soldier walked with a limp, some because of their wounds, others because they had been unable to secure replacements for worn-out shoes. To make life even more miserable, they were harassed constantly by the militia of Bladen County under Colonel Alexander Lillington. Stragglers who were not able to keep up with the main British column were picked off one by one. In all, Cornwallis lost about thirty-five soldiers to Lillington's men between Cross Creek and Wilmington. Never did a place look so good to these British soldiers as did Wilmington when they limped into town on April 7, 1781.

CHAPTER VII

WAR IN THE COASTAL PLAINS

The town of Wilmington was important to the success of Lord Cornwallis's campaign. While he was pursuing Greene through the western part of North Carolina, things had been happening in the region along the coast. On January 28, 1781, a fleet of eighteen vessels flying the British flag dropped anchor in the Cape Fear River near Wilmington. On board were 450 redcoats under the command of Major James Craig.

In 1781 there were approximately 200 houses in Wilmington, and its population was almost 1,000. The populace, however, were civilians, unprepared to fight or defend their homes. There was no opposition as Craig took possession of the town. He immediately put his soldiers to work throwing up fortifications around the town. Patrols were sent out to round up all the prominent Whigs in the neighborhood. Some of the natives tried to escape. Thomas Bloodworth, the tax collector, loaded everything pertaining to his office on board a small vessel and dispatched it up the Cape Fear River. Craig's soldiers, after a twenty-mile ride across country, caught up with this boat, captured it, and then burned it.

Other patrols, mounted on the best horses of the Cape Fear region, rode constantly. Cornelius Harnett, who lived just outside of Wilmington, attempted to flee. He fell ill in Anson County, and there he was captured by Craig's men. Some say that his death soon after this was the result of his ill-treatment by the British. General John Ashe suffered a similar fate. He hid out in a swamp, but he was betrayed to the enemy by one of his servants. When he attempted to escape, he was shot in the leg. Soon afterwards he died of smallpox. Other leading Whigs were captured, some by the Tories, who turned them over to the British in Wilmington.

With the British soldiers in the area to protect them, the Tories became bolder. To keep them under control, General Alexander Lillington called out the militia. He fortified a position at Heron Bridge, about ten miles up the Northeast River from Wilmington. Near the end of February, Craig made a surprise attack upon Lillington and his militia, but he could not dislodge the stubborn rebels. After two days of bombarding the American position, Craig gave up and returned to Wilmington, leaving Lillington and his men in command of Heron Bridge.

There were others in and about Wilmington who annoyed the enemy. A story is told about a gunsmith named Bloodworth. He used to take his favorite rifle down to the Northeast River, across from the spot where the British soldiers brought their horses to water. Concealing himself in a hollow tree, Bloodworth waited patiently until one of the red-coated troopers came into range. It was only after several of the British soldiers had been killed that his hiding place was discovered. A detachment was sent across the river to capture this bold sniper, but Bloodworth made his escape.

Craig's men were working on the fortifications when Cornwallis's men marched into town on April 7th. The general immediately established his headquarters in one of the finer houses in town; the church building was put into use as a hospital for the sick and wounded.

Cornwallis spent much of his time over the planning table. Should he return to South Carolina to make another strike at Greene, or should he consolidate the meager victory he had won in North Carolina? His army was in no condition to fight another battle. On the other hand, Major General Phillips was in Virginia with an army of fresh troops. And Virginia, he thought, should be a tranquil and subdued state as a result of the ravages of the American turncoat, Benedict Arnold. Arnold had ranged over Virginia, plundering and pillaging as he rode. Virginia offered Cornwallis the prospect of fresh troops and new fame. He decided to march northward.

Cornwallis's army rested just a little over two weeks in Wilmington. When they marched out of town they were minus one of the persons who had been with them ever since the fall of Charleston. This was the former royal governor of North Carolina, Josiah Martin. Even so enthusiastic an optimist as Martin no longer could foresee the return of North Carolina to royal rule. Pleading illness, he boarded the first ship sailing from Wilmington to England.

Once again the red-coated army was on the move. Trudging along the rutted, sandy roads, they marched slowly and almost deliberately into Duplin County. The entire countryside was terrorized. Tories and other hangers-on, who followed the British army like a flight of vultures, plundered every farm and plantation along the way. Some homes roared up in a mass of flames and smoke-blackened chimneys marked the path of the marching column. Horses and cattle were driven off, and slaves were forced to come along with the army. Many Whigs loaded their families and most valuable possessions into wagons and hastened to a safer area.

Cornwallis met with no opposition until May 6, 1781. At Peacock's Bridge over Contentnea Creek (near Stantonsburg), were stationed 400 determined militia from Pitt County under Colonel James Gorham. Although these citizen soldiers were able to make a brief stand at the bridge, they were soon scattered when a cavalry charge was made by Tarleton and his men. Tarleton then was sent on across the Tar River to scout and disperse any Whigs who later might cause trouble. At Swift Creek and Fishing Creek, small detachments of Americans were bold enough to challenge him, but they were dispersed with little trouble.

Tarleton received word that a fairly large group of North Carolina militia was assembling at Halifax. By travelling across country and approaching the town from an unexpected direction he was able to surprise them. The ensuing fight was short. Thundering horses and flashing sabers put the disorganized militia to flight. In this brief skirmish the British suffered a loss of three men and several horses. Some of the bolder militia began to throw up earthworks on the far side of the Roanoke River. When British soldiers approached the stream, they were treated to a storm of musket shots from the other shore. The militiamen made such a nuisance of themselves that a small force was sent across the river to drive them out.

The citizens of Halifax were subjected to many indignities after the troops of Cornwallis occupied the town. Homes were plundered of valuables and the people insulted. At one time the situation was so much out of control that Cornwallis courtmartialled and executed a sergeant and a dragoon for outrages for which they had been responsible.

In late May, Charles, First Marquis Cornwallis, marched out of North Carolina on the road to Petersburg in Virginia. He had spent over three months in the State and had accomplished little. In late January he had entered North Carolina with a veteran army; he now was leaving its borders with but a shadow of his once fine fighting machine. He had fought one major battle, for which he had made a hollow claim of victory. At both the Cowpens and Guilford Court House he had lost some of the best soldiers under his command. It was the loss of these soldiers that was partly responsible for Cornwallis's defeat and surrender at Yorktown, Virginia, October 19, 1781.

Craig continued his activity at Wilmington and vicinity. He offered rewards for enlistments in the British service and, when the Whigs made no response, he encouraged the Tories to persecute them. He constructed outlying fortifications as far away as Rutherford's Mills (near present-day Burgaw). When General Alexander Lillington attempted to call out the militia in Onslow County, detachments of dragoons were sent to break up the assembly.

Tories in eastern North Carolina continued their strikes against the despised Whigs. Some Whigs were forced to flee from their homes and hide in the swamps. When possible, they struck back. For instance, when one McLaurin Colvill was appointed a colonel in the loyalist militia, his house was surrounded on a dark night by the Whigs who killed him.

Pitched battles were not unknown. When the Tory "flying army" of Colonels Hector McNeil and Davean Ray drove off the stock of the Whigs of Cumberland County and then tried to force them to give up their arms, they met resistance. Colonel Thomas Wade of Anson County called out his militia regiment. Smaller groups from Montgomery and Richmond counties joined him.

On Saturday night, August 4, 1781, Wade met the Tories at Beatty's Bridge on Drowning Creek. A sharp skirmish followed, with rifles cracking on both sides of the creek until nearly midnight. Soon the Tories had enough fighting and retreated, their losses amounting to twelve men killed and fifteen wounded. None of Wade's men had been killed, and only four had suffered wounds.

Most of the time, however, Major Craig managed to keep the Whigs of eastern North Carolina off balance. He announced that he would seize and sell the property of all those who resisted British measures. By August 1, 1781, he declared, all the inhabitants of the area were to come into Wilmington and take the oath of allegiance to George III. If they refused, they would be suspected as being enemies of the King, and would be in danger of having their property confiscated and losing their lives. Few Whigs came in to take the oath. On August 1st, Craig marched out on an expedition to punish all those who had not complied with his requirements.

At Rock Creek (sometimes called "Rockfish" and near present-day Wallace) he was opposed briefly by the patriot militia of Duplin County under Colonel James Kenan. The engagement lasted only a short while because Kenan's men soon exhausted their ammunition. They retreated. None of these courageous Duplin County men lost their lives, but about twenty or thirty were taken by the British cavalry who pursued them after the skirmish.

For ten days Craig remained in Duplin County. Many of those who refused to take the oath saw the torch applied to their homes. Some 300 loyalists came in and joined the British. When Craig's column marched towards New Bern, small groups of mounted Whigs made nuisances of themselves by darting in for a sudden strike. This was all they could do. They did not possess the ammunition to make a stand.

Around 2:00 P.M., on Sunday, August 19, 1781, Craig's force arrived in New Bern, his trail marked by the ruins of Whig plantations. Among the homes that had been burned was that belonging to General Alexander Lillington. Some of the loyal natives of New Bern welcomed the British; some of the Whigs took pot shots at them as they entered the town. One of the first things Craig had his men do was to destroy all the rigging of the ships tied up along the waterfront. Much of the cargo on board these vessels was destroyed, including some 3,000 barrels of salt. This was especially disastrous, for in those days before electric refrigeration, salt was one of the main items used in the preservation of meat.

Several of the leading citizens of New Bern had fled at the approach of the British. Dr. Alexander Gaston tried to make his escape by rowing across Trent River. A British officer coldly shot him down before the eyes of Gaston's horrified wife.

On Tuesday, August 21st, after only two days in town, Craig left New Bern and marched towards Kinston. Along the road there was a brief skirmish with the militia of Colonel James Gorham, but they were soon driven off. The British camped on the spot and burned four houses in the neighborhood, including the home of General Bryan.

Craig's plan to march farther into the interior of the State was interrupted by word that the Continental troops of General "Mad Anthony" Wayne had entered North Carolina on their way to join General Greene. The British hurriedly turned south

Lord Cornwallis surrenders his troops to General George Washington, October 19, 1781, at Yorktown, Virginia.

towards Wilmington. From Craig's point of view, it had been a most successful raid. He was satisfied that the rebels had received their just punishment for their refusal to come in and take the oath of allegiance. He had been able to inflict this punishment at a cost of only thirty men killed, wounded, or taken prisoner.

The Tories did not share Craig's sense of success. Just as soon as the British had marched too far to offer them protection, the Whigs came out of hiding and began to gather in an effort to crush the loyalists.

There was a full-scale battle at Elizabeth Town where the Tory colonel, John Slingsby, had been holding a number of Whig prisoners. About 150 men from Bladen County cautiously approached the town. Under cover of darkness they forded the river. Just before dawn they launched their attack. The sudden assault threw the Tories into a panic. Large numbers of them, rushing headlong through the dim light, fell into a deep ravine. So many either leaped or stumbled into this ditch that it has since become known as "Tories' Hole." The Whigs quickly collected all the arms and stores in town and retired to the other side of the river. Only one of their men had been wounded. Nineteen Tories were killed, wounded, or taken prisoner. Slingsby was among these, and later died of his wounds.

The Tories retaliated quickly. Colonel David Fanning, one of the most ruthless and daring of all the Tory leaders, hastened to the aid of the force at Elizabeth Town. He arrived too late. He did receive word that the men of Colonel Thomas Wade were encamped on Drowning Creek. Marching towards these Whigs, he was joined along the way by the Tories of Colonel Hector McNeil. Together, they surprised Wade in a narrow section of Raft Swamp. They charged Wade's position just before noon. The rebels fired, aiming at the charging horses. Eighteen dropped at the first volley. The Tories dismounted and advanced on foot, firing as they came. When they were within twenty-five yards of Wade's troops, the Whigs broke and ran. Fanning's men quickly remounted and took up the pursuit. Fifty-four prisoners were taken. Twenty-three Whigs lay dead on the battlefield. The Tories captured a total of 250 horses. This victory in Raft Swamp more than compensated for the Tory rout at Elizabeth Town.

This demonstration of strength by the Tories was one of the reasons why General Griffith Rutherford led his troops into the area. The general had been captured at the Battle of Camden and had spent much of the intervening time as a prisoner-of-war in Florida. When he was exchanged he again took the field against the enemy. He issued a call for volunteers and, after two weeks of training and organizing the men, moved towards Wilmington on October 1st.

In the neighborhood of that town, he deployed his troops over a large area and slowly began to close in upon the town. Several attacks by the Tories were brushed off. Like a great hand slowly squeezing an orange, he kept moving his men nearer and nearer to Wilmington.

Then suddenly, the picture completely changed. On November 17, 1781, Light Horse Harry Lee stopped by Rutherford's camp. He was returning from Virginia on his way to rejoin General Greene in South Carolina. Lee bore news—earthshaking news! He gleefully reported that on October 19, 1781, at Yorktown in Virginia, Lord Cornwallis had surrendered to General Washington. Rutherford's camp went wild. Shouts, war whoops, and cheers rang through the forests. Valuable gunpowder was wasted as muskets were fired again and again in wild celebration.

There was no time for a long celebration. Good news followed fast on the heels of good news. Reports came that Craig was evacuating Wilmington. Rutherford immediately moved his troops closer to the town. On November 18, 1781, the North Carolinians marched jauntily into Wilmington. Still in sight were the troopships transporting Craig's soldiers. The last British redcoat had left North Carolina soil. Now there were only the Tories.

CHAPTER VIII

PEACE

Military activity had not been restricted to eastern North Carolina and Virginia. In South Carolina, General Greene had fought another battle. In this engagement at Eutaw Springs, there were a considerable number of North Carolinians under the command of General Jethro Sumner. Many of these same men had seen action at Guilford Court House; now they were better trained and better equipped. At Eutaw Springs they fought bravely and suffered heavy losses. Their gallantry in battle drew the highest praise from General Greene.

Several political changes had also occurred in the government of North Carolina. In June, 1781, the General Assembly had met at Wake Courthouse and elected Thomas Burke of Hillsboro to succeed Governor Abner Nash. Burke had long been active in the revolutionary movement, and had for some time represented North Carolina in the Continental Congress. One of his primary concerns after he became the chief executive was that of keeping the Tories quiet and under control of the Whigs. He investigated the most troublesome areas in the State. In September Burke returned to Hillsboro, determined to organize an extensive campaign against the loyalists.

Not far from Hillsboro, a small detachment of North Carolina militia under the command of General John Butler was encamped on the south bank of the Haw River. Burke had just arrived in Hillsboro when he received word that the two notorious Tories, David Fanning and Hector McNeil, were on their way to make a surprise attack upon Butler. A rider was sent galloping off to warn Butler.

Burke was mistaken. Butler was not the primary objective of Fanning and McNeil. They had their eye on a bigger prize—the governor himself! The Tories approached Hillsboro in the blackness of night. The next morning, Wednesday, September 12, 1781, a heavy fog blanketed the area. Fanning's men crept quietly through the mist, entering the town from every side. The townspeople were not aware of the presence of the raiders until there was a sudden burst of musket fire. Doors were hurriedly bolted as men rushed for their firearms to defend their homes and families.

Governor Burke's home was surrounded. Burke put up a vigorous defense, although his only support came from his aide-de-camp, Captain Reid, an orderly sergeant, and John Huske, his secretary. Despite their efforts, this little group was soon overpowered, and the Tories had captured the Governor of North Carolina! Other prisoners were taken. The town jail was broken open and about thirty loyalist prisoners were released. The jailors then were locked in their own prison. A number of homes in the town were plundered of their valuables. About two o'clock in the afternoon, the Tories marched out of town, carrying their prisoner with them.

Alexander Mebane rode swiftly to warn General Butler. The governor must be rescued. Near Lindley's Mill on Cane Creek, some eighteen miles from Hillsboro, Butler prepared an ambush for the men of Fanning and McNeil. The Tories, tramping noisily along the trail, were unaware of the presence of their enemies until the opening volley threw them into a panic. At the first fire Colonel Hector McNeil fell from his horse with three musket balls in his body. The Tories scurried back out of range, but were soon rallied by Fanning.

Fanning first sent off his prisoners for safekeeping. Then he led one group across the creek upstream from the scene of the action. He circled around through the trees, and his sudden appearance in the rear of the Whigs threw Butler's men into the greatest confusion. They recovered quickly and for the next four hours there was a running battle along Cane Creek. Butler and his militia eventually were forced to withdraw, leaving behind twenty-five killed, ninety wounded, and ten men captured by the enemy. Fanning lost twenty-seven killed and nearly ninety wounded. He was himself wounded in the left arm. He had lost so much blood that he was in no condition to march. His men hid him in the forest and continued on without him. Hurrying to Wilmington, they turned over Governor Burke to Major Craig. A short time later the governor was sent to Charleston. So long as Burke remained a prisoner of the British, Alexander Martin of Guilford County, the Speaker of the Senate, was the acting governor of North Carolina.

It was while Martin was acting in this capacity that news was received of Cornwallis's surrender at Yorktown (at a much earlier date than it had been heard by Rutherford's men at Wilmington). In late October, a trooper on his way with dispatches for General Greene told of the surrender when he stopped briefly in the town. Hillsboro went wild, with a celebration featuring parades, bonfires, and the firing of many guns. "We were all so elated," wrote one of the celebrants, "that the time elapsed in frolicking."

In late January, 1782, Governor Burke returned to Hillsboro. After he had been taken to Charleston, he had been paroled to James Island, just outside that town. A parole meant that he had given his word of honor that he would not escape. In return for that promise, he was allowed to go anywhere he pleased on James Island. Also on the island were a number of renegade Tories who had taken a particular dislike to Burke. On one occasion they had fired into the house where he was staying, killing one of the governor's companions and wounding another. The British authorities paid little attention to Burke's protests. Feeling that his life would be in even greater danger should he stay on the island, he escaped and made his way back to North Carolina.

Breaking a parole reflected upon one's honor and integrity. Many people strongly criticised Governor Burke for his action. Other prominent people came to his defense. General Greene became involved in a long dispute with the British commander at Charleston over his treatment of Burke. The governor paid little attention to his critics and busied himself with the duties of his office.

The war, for all practical purposes, was over with the surrender of Cornwallis. Yet, there remained the problem of the Tories. David Fanning recovered from his wound and resumed his operations in the Hillsboro district, terrorizing many, and killing some, of the inhabitants. Nevertheless, his career was fast drawing to a close. By May, 1782, Fanning fled to South Carolina, and eventually removed to Nova Scotia where he lived the remaining years of his life.

In April, 1782, Alexander Martin was elected the fourth governor of the State of North Carolina. A difficult task lay before him. He found himself the chief executive of a state with no money in its treasury, with no permanent capital at which he could establish a seat of government, and whose lands had been ravaged by marching armies. There was the very great problem of supplying General Greene with men and food. Even after the

British evacuated Charleston on December 14, 1782, Greene was required to maintain a small army in the field. Most of the soldiers were released from military duty, but it was not until April, 1783, that the last North Carolina soldier was discharged.

That same April saw Governor Martin lay before the General Assembly a copy of the peace treaty between the American colonies and Great Britain. This was the document which stated that North Carolina and the twelve other American colonies were now "free, sovereign and independent states." The war was now over officially.

The American Revolution in North Carolina had contained all the phases of a bitter civil war. It had seen the transition of North Carolina from a royal colony to a sovereign state. The war had been fought under the guidance of the State's first four governors: Richard Caswell, Abner Nash, Thomas Burke, and Alexander Martin.

A Constitution for the new State had been adopted which had provided the basis for a new system of government and law. Politics and political divisions had arisen among the people, each party wanting to govern the new State in the manner it thought best.

The greatest political division had been between the Tories and the Whigs. This split had the unhappy result of many families breaking up, and sometimes had turned father against son and brother against brother. Members of the same family had fought on different sides in the same battles. In the beginning, the Whigs had attempted to win the loyalists over to their side; when persuasion failed, they turned to sterner measures. Laws were passed exiling Tories from the State (many did leave), and their property was taken from them.

Some people of more peaceful inclinations did not take up arms for either side. There were people like the Quakers, whose religious beliefs did not approve the taking of life. Equally peaceful were the Moravians of Salem and, when they refused to favor either group, they were persecuted by Whigs and Tories alike.

One of the greatest problems of the war had been financial. North Carolina, as had most of the colonies, won her independence by fighting a war with practically an empty treasury. The decline of foreign trade had eliminated a market in which the people could sell their products and little new money found its way into the State. The great quantity of paper money printed during the war so decreased in value that by 1783, a soldier was receiving the equivalent of six cents a month for serving his country's cause! The scarcity of money made taxes difficult to collect and eventually they were paid "in kind," with such produce as corn, wheat, flour, pork, beef, etc.

The war had seen the rise of a great deal of manufacturing in the home. Stores early had sold out their stocks and, when trade declined, there was nothing else brought in for them to place on their shelves. When a shipload of goods did enter port, its cargo usually went to supply the army. Suits and dresses made of homespun became the style and often homemade shoes cramped aching feet.

There also had been the problem of the army. Quotas had to be raised for the Continental army. Supplies had to be furnished the men in the field. Militia had to be organized, trained, and equipped. Although the militia troops were never long in the field, most of them marched out against the enemy at one time or another. It has been estimated that nearly 22,000 North Carolinians (continental and militia) saw service during the War of the Revolution.

The State had even attempted the organization of a navy. However, there never was a very large fleet and its primary purpose had been to protect the ships coming into Ocracoke Inlet. Altogether, three ships were launched, the "Pennsylvania Farmer," the "Washington," and the "Caswell." A number of privateers put to sea from North Carolina ports. These were privately-owned ships armed with cannon. They were authorized by the State to capture British merchant ships, which they were allowed to sell, keeping a percentage of the proceeds. The best known privateers operating out of North Carolina bore names such as, the "Sturdy Beggar," "Chatham," "Ballona," "Rambeau," "Fanny," "Betsey," "General Nash," "Lydia," and the "Nancy."

An enemy army had ravaged the State. Homes had become smoke-blackened ruins because their owners would not support the British King. Armies, both American and British, had lived off the land, consuming the crops, sometimes before they were even ready for harvest.

Some of the most promising young men of North Carolina had died on the field of battle. Others returned home, crippled for life.

To rebuild and heal old wounds: These were the great tasks facing the people of North Carolina in the spring of 1783. It was to take time and much hard work. But it could be done by a sovereign state among the United States of America.

And they were free!